T0282292

NEW TESTAMENT
EVERYDAY BIBLE STUDIES

NEW TESTAMENT
EVERYDAY BIBLE STUDIES

1 & 2 PETER AND JUDE

STAYING FAITHFUL TO THE GOSPEL

SCOT MCKNIGHT

QUESTIONS WRITTEN BY
BECKY CASTLE MILLER

 Harper*Christian*
Resources

New Testament Everyday Bible Study Series: 1 & 2 Peter and Jude
© 2024 by Scot McKnight

Published in Grand Rapids, Michigan, by HarperChristian Resources.
HarperChristian Resources is a registered trademark of HarperCollins
Christian Publishing, Inc.

Requests for information should be sent to customercare@harpercollins.com.

ISBN 978-0-310-12957-8 (softcover)
ISBN 978-0-310-12958-5 (ebook)

HarperChristian Resources titles may be purchased in bulk for church,
business, fundraising, or ministry use. For information, please e-mail
ResourceSpecialist@ChurchSource.com.

First Printing August 2024 / Printed in the United States of America

24 25 26 27 28 LBC 5 4 3 2 1

CONTENTS

JUDE

For Northern's DMin students

GENERAL INTRODUCTION

Christians make a claim for the Bible not made of any other book. Or, since the Bible is a library shelf of many authors, it's a claim we make of no other shelf of books. We claim that God worked in each of the authors as they were writing so that what was scratched on papyrus expressed what God wanted communicated to the people of God. Which makes the New Testament (NT) a book unlike any other book. Which is why Christians are reading the NT almost two thousand years later with great delight. These books have the power to instruct us and to rebuke us and to correct us and to train us to walk with God every day. We read these books because God speaks to us in them.

Developing a routine of reading the Bible with an open heart, a receptive mind, and a flexible will is the why of the *New Testament Everyday Bible Studies*. But not every day will be the same. Some days we pause and take it in and other days we stop and repent and lament and open ourselves to God's restoring graces. No one word suffices for what the Bible does to us. In fact, the Bible's view of the Bible can be found by reading Psalm 119, the longest chapter in the Bible with 176 verses! It is a meditation on eight terms for what the Bible is and what the Bible does to those who listen and read it. Its laws (*torah*) instruct us, its laws (*mishpat*) order us, its statutes direct us, its precepts inform us, its decrees guide us, its commands compel us, its words speak to us, and its promises comfort us, and it is no wonder that the author can sum all eight up as the "way" (119:3). Each of those terms still speaks to what happens when we open our minds to the Word of God.

Every day with the Bible then is new because our timeless and timely God communes with us in our daily lives in our world and in our time. Just as God spoke to Jesus in Galilee and Paul in Ephesus and John on Patmos. These various contexts help us hear God in our context so the *New Testament Everyday Bible Studies* will often delve into contexts.

Most of us now have a Bible on our devices. We may well have several translations available to us everywhere we go every day. To hear those words, we are summoned by God to open the Bible, to attune our hearts to God, and to listen to what God says. My prayer is that these daily study guides will help each of us become daily Bible readers attentive to the mind of God.

INTRODUCTION: READING THE BOOKS OF 1 & 2 PETER AND JUDE

At age sixteen, Peter could never have guessed what his life would become. He grew up in Galilee, fished in the Sea of Galilee, and knew dozens in his family's circle. A short biography of Peter may help each of us as we read 1–2 Peter. As a young adult he was called to drop the fishing to follow Jesus with his brother. He became the "first among equals" among the twelve disciples. They were all "sent" out by Jesus, which is why we know them today as apostles (sent ones). He accompanied Jesus, listened to Jesus, observed Jesus, and did his best to do what Jesus did. His failures became a matter of public record: he sunk in the water when trying to walk on water, and he failed miserably to own up to being a close follower of Jesus during Jesus' trials. But Jesus forgave him, restored him, and commissioned him all over again. So much for the story of Peter in the Gospels.

Peter was at Pentecost. He preached the first Pentecost Day sermon. He was for a short while the go-to apostle in Jerusalem for the suddenly growing church. The authorities learned about him and ordered him to stop publicly claiming Jesus as the Messiah. He didn't; he suffered for it; he was pushed from Jerusalem. In a famous vision of unclean foods and animals and then in a just-as-famous incident in Caesarea (by the sea) he proclaimed the gospel to a gentile named Cornelius. Not long after he was in Jerusalem where he was queried by the "circumcised believers" (Acts 11:2) about how kosher his gospel and practices were. He witnessed to what happened; they could not deny the mighty acts of God. Back in Jerusalem, Peter was arrested once again, and he was liberated from prison by a miracle. Jerusalem's Christian leaders held a conference about how much of the law of Moses these new gentile converts were to observe. Peter gave a short summary of watching God's movement among the gentiles, and the leaders sent out a letter requiring a gentile minimum when it came to observing the laws of Moses. They ferreted out the four laws specifically given for gentiles in the Land. Those laws are found listed in Acts 15:16–18 and they derive from Leviticus 17–18.

What we know from this point on about Peter is not much. What we do know is that Peter, like his parallel but sometimes contentious friend (Paul), became a missionary in Asia Minor. He seemed to have planted churches throughout Asia Minor. We also know he was in Rome, from where (presumably) two letters in the New Testament were written (see more below at the introduction to 2 Peter).

First Peter advocates for the believers in the "provinces of Pontus, Galatia, Cappadocia, Asia and Bithynia" (1:1) a way of life for believers in Jesus under the rule of Rome. Peter's approach to the Christian life is not unlike Paul's. He begins with salvation (1:3–12) before proceeding to holiness (1:13–2:3) for the church (2:4–10). At this point, Peter turns to the center of this letter, and this section is so long that one is led to think this is the heart of Peter's approach to living in the empire according to one's status and social location. After a brief theoretical statement (2:11–12), Peter turns to life before the government (2:13–17), to slaves (2:18–25), to wives (3:1–6), to husbands (3:7), and then finally to the collective of believers in all locations (3:8–12). That final set of instructions morphs naturally into instructions about how to handle the threat and experience of suffering for following Jesus (3:13–4:19). Perhaps 3:8–4:19 was an interruption to addressing the social location of his audience. Peter addresses another social location when he instructs the elders (5:1–11). He signs off in 5:12–14, using an early Jewish and Christian trope for Rome, namely, calling it Babylon.

Shively Smith, in her important study of the diaspora way of life for the audience of 1 Peter, has discovered in this letter "a balancing act between integration and segregation, presence and difference, conformity and distinction" (Smith, *Strangers to Family*, 45). Following this theme, she sketches very helpfully the following practices that distinguish Christians from their environment, with these practices forming Christian identity and family kinships (45–59):

1. No idol worship
2. Baptism and creeds
3. Preaching
4. Prayer
5. Hospitality and staying sober

It has been said often that the fundamental lines in the sand for believers in the Roman empire separated them from idolatry and immorality. Peter drew those lines too.

Second Peter strikes the reader as far less pastoral in tone and more strident in expression. Some false teachers are in view, and Peter describes them in strong, even loathsome terms. These false teachers deny the second coming (1:16–18; 3:4–10) and break down common Christian moral practices (2:2, 10, 13, 18–22). Another tone emerges because

3

Peter appears to be on the verge of dying, making 2 Peter a bit of a farewell letter (1:14). In fact, many think 2 Peter not only borrows from Jude, but that this letter may not have been written by Peter but by one who followed his teachings carefully. Jude bears many similarities to 2 Peter, both in tone and content. But each letter has its own distinctives as our daily reflections will show.

WORKS CITED IN THE STUDY GUIDE

(Throughout the Guide you will find the author's name and title, as noted in this book listing, with page numbers whenever I cite something from it):

Dennis Edwards, *1 Peter* (Story of God Bible Commentary; Grand Rapids: Zondervan, 2017). [Edwards, *1 Peter*]

Larry George, "2 Peter," in *True to Our Native Land: An African American New Testament Commentary* (ed. Brian K. Blount; Minneapolis: Fortress, 2007), 488–495. [George, "2 Peter"]

Catherine Gonsalus González, *1 & 2 Peter and Jude* (Belief: A Theological Commentary on the Bible; Louisville: Westminster John Knox, 2010). Cited by book: [Gonzalez *1 Peter, 2 Peter,* or *Jude*]

Joel B. Green, *1 Peter* (Two Horizons New Testament Commentary; Grand Rapids: Wm. B. Eerdmans, 2007). [Green, *1 Peter*]

Scot McKnight, *1 Peter* (NIV Application Commentary; Grand Rapids: Zondervan, 1996). I assume the privilege of reworking what

I wrote nearly thirty years ago without always citing it. [McKnight, *1 Peter*]

Scot McKnight, *2 Peter* and *Jude* Eerdmans Commentary on the Bible (ed. James D.G. Dunn, John Rogerson; Grand Rapids: Wm. B. Eerdmans, 2003), 1504–1534. [McKnight, *2 Peter* or *Jude*]

Scot McKnight, *The Second Testament: A New Translation* (Downers Grove: IVP Academic, 2023). [McKnight, *Second Testament*]

Pheme Perkins, *First and Second Peter, James, and Jude* (Interpretation; Louisville: John Knox, 1995). [Perkins, *First Peter, Second Peter, James,* or *Jude*]

Shively T.J. Smith, *Strangers to Family: Diaspora and 1 Peter's Invention of God's Household* (Waco, Texas: Baylor University Press, 2016). [Smith, *Strangers to Family*]

1 PETER

WHO ARE THESE PEOPLE?

1 Peter 2:11–12

¹¹ Dear friends, I urge you, as foreigners and exiles, to abstain from sinful desires, which wage war against your soul. ¹² Live such good lives among the pagans that, though they accuse you of doing wrong, they may see your good deeds and glorify God on the day he visits us.

Special Note to the Reader: I am starting this study with 1 Peter 2:11–12 because these thematic verses express his approach to the Christian life in the Roman empire. Peter wrote this to instruct believers on how they should conduct themselves in a world that was not hospitable to their way of life. His pastoral hope was for them to be (1) faithful to Jesus and (2) effective in evangelism. These believers learned they were members of two worlds: the empire of Rome and the kingdom of God.

One travels a long distance between Peter's "Dear friends" (or "Loved ones" in *Second Testament*) and his terms for the believers in Asia Minor: "foreigners and exiles." Though many have understood these terms as no more than metaphors for life-as-a-pilgrimage, these two terms describe their *social* condition. One speaks of the intimacy of family,

9

friendship, and siblingship, and the other the rugged realities of the social location of these believers. Both of these terms have been translated with the same English term "exiles." I prefer the translation of 2:11 as "exiles and temporary residents" (*Second Testament*), which means I translate 1:1 with "elect temporary residents." One term in 2:11, *paroikos*, refers to residents without the legal protection of citizenship or belonging, while the second term, *parepidēmos*, points at residents who remain in a location for a short period. For the sake of boldness, I suggest we think of them as migrant workers rather than the more comfortable simile of life on earth as a journey or pilgrimage to heaven (discussed fully in McKnight, *1 Peter*, 47–51). "Think factory workers and undocumented farm or domestic workers; think sanitation workers, caretakers for the elderly; think (dare I say it?) sex workers—the people we see every day, or maybe we look past them, but as a society we depend on them nonetheless" (Davis, *The Luminous Word*, 308). You might be surprised by Ellen Davis's words but think again. The past of these believers was not squeaky clean. Many were victims. Many experienced generational poverty and marginalization. They found Jesus, they found community, and together they were chasing a life of holiness in the empire, which was their challenge and the reason for Peter's letter.

There is nothing in 2:11, or in 1:1 (in our next passage), suggesting these terms are anything but literal descriptions of a social location, nor is there anything suggesting they are mere metaphors. Dennis Edwards says it perfectly: "people on the margins have little power and influence in society. Yet they may still make a profound impact on the world when they are able to persevere and live according to the ways of the Lord Jesus" (Edwards, *1 Peter*, 28).

How, then, did they get to these locations? We don't know for sure, but what we do know is that an abundance of Jews lived in the diaspora outside Jerusalem, Judea, or Galilee. So, perhaps they chose to move because of family. Paul's family lived in Tarsus in Cilicia, west of Cappadocia. Perhaps they moved from Galilee for work, which one early Christian source says happened. Perhaps, because they were Jewish or foreigners or Christians, they were pushed out of one location and moved to these locations. Perhaps some of them were at Pentecost and returned home. Perhaps, because they were Christians, they fled persecution. (This letter has lots to say about suffering.) Perhaps they were alienated in their own locations because of their faith or heritage. Most likely these believers, or at least some of them, had been persons of lower social standing prior to meeting Jesus and remained so, or were lowered in social status because of their faith. What we know is that these two terms direct our attention to Christians living at the level of subsistence (see more in Sidebar). Joel Green puts it like this: "First Peter is addressed to folks who do not belong, who eke out their lives on the periphery of acceptable society, whose deepest loyalties and inclinations do not line up very well with what matters most in the world in which they live. This is not the sort of life that most people find attractive" (Green, *1 Peter*, 18).

What does it mean, then, to follow the way of Jesus in their condition? That's an important question to answer for reading 1 Peter.

Social Location Matters

Estimates for what percentage of the population fit into which level are necessarily approximate, but one can get a lasting impression with the following.

Level 1	0.04%	Imperial elites
Level 2	1.00%	Regional, provincial elites
Level 3	1.76%	Municipal elites
Level 4	7%	Moderate surplus resources
Level 5	22%	Stable, but near subsistence level
Level 6	40%	Subsistence, often below minimum
Level 7	28%	Below subsistence

Approximately ninety percent, perhaps slightly less, of the population of these provinces lived near, at, or below the subsistence level. Poverty reigned in agrarian economies. The agenda for most people was resources, an abundant harvest, a good year as an artisan. The clamor of crowds broke out of these subsistence conditions. Their clamor spoke the dialect of trauma. Life on the edge of subsistence traumatizes generationally.

To put muscle and skin and hair on these levels, the various occupations, vocations, or professions look like this:

Level 1	Roman officials, occasional retainers, and freedpersons
Level 2	Provincial officials, retainers, retired military
Level 3	Wealthy who do not hold offices, some freedpersons, retainers, veterans, merchants
Level 4	Some merchants, traders, freedpersons, artisans, veterans

Level 5   Most merchants, traders, wage earners,
           artisans, large shop owners, farm families
Level 6   Small farm families, laborers both
           skilled and unskilled, employed artisans,
           wage earners, most merchants and
           traders, small shop and tavern owners
Level 7   Some farm families, unattached
           widows, orphans, beggars, disabled,
           unskilled day laborers, prisoners

The believers addressed by Peter mostly resided in Levels 5, 6, and 7. What matters, and this cannot be ignored, is the numbers. Levels 5–7 comprise ninety percent of the population. A disproportionate number in Levels 1–4 resided in the big cities, like Antioch or Ephesus. Most were on the margins.

HOW TO LIVE?

Peter's approach to life for these marginalized people is as old as any moral teaching in history and as relevant right now wherever you are: avoid bad behaviors, do good behaviors. So, they are (1) to avoid "fleshy desires" (more about this at 1:13–2:3) and (2) to live a publicly "beautiful" life (*Second Testament*). One of the biggest challenges of the earliest Christians was to learn how to live as followers of Jesus in a way that (1) did not destroy the Jesus movement by rebelling against the machine and that (2) remained faithful to the way of Jesus. If Revelation becomes the paradigm of dissident discipleship and resistance to the way of the empire (Babylon), Peter offers another approach to fit his audience. They were to live publicly beautiful, or attractive, lives. He uses a very special word here. He says they are to practice "good deeds," or "good works." This captures one's public life (cf. Matthew 5:16) and does not refer to what Paul means by "good works" when he is critical of them.

What is even more vital to Peter's strategy is his theory of *doing good*. The Greek terms at work are built on *agathos* (good) and *poi-* (do). Please read each of these verses, and I italicize the important words that translate the above Greek term.

> . . . governors, who are sent by him to punish those who do wrong and to commend those who *do right* (2:14).

> For it is God's will that *by doing good* you should silence the ignorant talk of foolish people (2:15).

> But how is it to your credit if you receive a beating for doing wrong and endure it? But if you suffer *for doing good* and you endure it, this is commendable before God (2:20).

> Like Sarah . . . You are her daughters if you *do what is right* and do not give way to fear (3:6).

> For it is better, if it is God's will, to suffer *for doing good* than for doing evil (3:17).

> So then, those who suffer according to God's will should commit themselves to their faithful Creator and continue *to do good* (4:19).

We could run out of space quickly here, so I want to reduce this to the basics: the terms Peter uses describe public acts of benefaction for the common good. His concern is not so much that they are to be good citizens of the empire or even of the local community. Being nice people is not enough. The deeper concern is to be people of good character who do what is good for others. That first verse cited from 2:14 makes an astounding point: what is being done by the believers has the potential to gain approval and public honor from political authorities. What would these benefactions look like? I quote from an expert on this theme, Bruce Winter:

> Benefactions included supplying grain in times of necessity by diverting the grain-carrying ships to the city, forcing down the price by selling it in the market below the asking rate, erecting public buildings or adorning old buildings with marble revetments such as in Corinth, refurbishing the theatre, widening roads, helping in the construction of public utilities, going on embassies to gain privileges for the city, and helping in the city in times of civil upheaval. (Winter, *Seek the Welfare of the City*, 37)

As we read through this letter, we need to keep in mind two elements that shine forth from this thematic passage in chapter two: first, that these believers are at the lower end of the social ladder and, second, they are to engage as they can in public benefactions. How can they do so as the poor? By participating in the benefactions as laborers or in any way they can establish a good reputation for the church that brings glory to God (2:12).

WHO ARE THEY?

As mentioned in the Introduction, the churches of Asia Minor were experiencing suffering for their faith. Whenever a group experiences social pressure like this, the group

15

develops strategies for cohesion and survival. In a theory developed long ago but still of much value, Bernard Siegel detailed four strategies:

1. a cadre of leadership is formed;
2. they marry within the group, something called endogamy;
3. the group forms cultural identity symbols;
4. and the youth are educated or discipled into the group's way of life. (Siegel, "Defensive Structuring")

Today's passage embodies this theory because the community of believers was experiencing stress and opposition (2:12: "accuse you of doing wrong" unjustly). The training of youth and formation of leadership emerge in one single verse. At 5:5 Peter urges the younger men to live consistently with the ways of the wiser, older men, and in this way, he affirms leadership (5:1–4) and education. Chapter three's concerns with husbands and wives, not the least the believing partners, illustrates endogamy. Their most important cultural symbol may be the names Peter mentions in today's reading: they are "exiles and temporary residents." They know where they actually belong (kingdom of God), and that this world is not the eternal city Rome claimed for itself.

This theoretical reflection yields deep insights for the letter: Peter is addressing a group of Christ followers who are marginalized but identified with some of the most glowing terms in the whole Bible (2:9–10). Even more, they are following Jesus, the Messiah and Lord and Savior and Living Stone and Great Shepherd. As followers they are also siblings. All this yields a community that is a family and a community that recognizes them regardless of their location on the social ladder (2:13–3:12). This letter will bounce how to live off who they are over and over.

QUESTIONS FOR REFLECTION AND APPLICATION

1. How does Peter expect the believers to live in two worlds at once (the Roman Empire and the kingdom of God)?

2. What does "do good" mean to Peter?

3. How does it change your perspective to think of the audience of this letter as migrant workers rather than spiritual pilgrims?

4. In what ways can these poor believers participate in benefaction, an activity often associated with the wealthy upper class?

5. What does it mean to you to live a "publicly beautiful" life today?

FOR FURTHER READING

Ellen Davis, *Preaching the Luminous Word: Biblical Sermons and Homiletical Essays* (with Austin McIver Dennis; Grand Rapids: Wm. B. Eerdmans, 2016).

Bernard Siegel, "Defensive Structuring and Environmental Stress," *American Journal of Sociology* 76 (1970), 11–32.

Bruce Winter, *Seek the Welfare of the City: Christians as Benefactors and Citizens* (Grand Rapids: Wm. B. Eerdmans, 1994).

GLOBAL WORDS
FOR A LOCAL LIFE

1 Peter 1:1–2

¹ *Peter, an apostle of Jesus Christ,*

To God's elect, exiles scattered throughout the provinces of Pontus, Galatia, Cappadocia, Asia and Bithynia, ² *who have been chosen according to the foreknowledge of God the Father, through the sanctifying work of the Spirit, to be obedient to Jesus Christ and sprinkled with his blood:*

Grace and peace be yours in abundance.

Both of the earliest churches' major apostles, Paul and Peter, had a challenge on their hands: how to get believers who lived in the Roman empire to live like Jesus and not like Romans. Peter, not unlike Paul, chose some global words for his readers and listeners. He was not writing theoretical theology. Instead, he chose to give pastoral wisdom for living the Christian way of life in one's own community.

His big words for a local life deserve special attention here, beginning with their *spiritual* condition. As Catherine González emphasizes, these believers (and we too) need to know *who* they (and we) are, and who they are becomes *whose* they (and we) are: God's redeemed people (González,

1 Peter, 12). They are **elect**, which translates from the Greek word *eklektos* from which we get our English term. This term connects all believers to Jesus, the precious Elect One (2:4, 6). Because we are "in" the Elect One, we become elect (2:9). Our election is to more than our salvation or deliverance. Our election makes us, as Peter will clarify, "a chosen people, a royal priesthood, a holy nation, God's special possession, that you may declare the praises of him who called you out of darkness into his wonderful light. Once you were not a people, but now you are the people of God; once you had not received mercy, but now you have received mercy" (2:9–10). The gentile believers, by their inclusion, expand the formerly more restricted covenant people of God, Israel.

That Peter's letter is sent from Pontus south to Galatia, east to Cappadocia, then all the way west to Asia and then back to the next-door neighbor of Pontus, that is, to Bithynia, suggests Peter's mission was every bit as widespread as Paul's, minus Greece. If we would follow Paul's words in Galatians 2:8, we would think Paul went to gentiles and Peter to Jews, but the facts counter that scheme. Paul began in synagogues, a mission as Jewish as it can get, and Peter's letter suggests beyond dispute that gentiles were in view in this letter (1 Peter 1:13–2:3).

As discussed at 2:11–12 in our previous reflection, the term "temporary residents" (*Second Testament*) or "**exiles**" (NIV) points to the social location of the believers. This set of Christian churches are "scattered throughout" a number of provinces of Asia Minor. The NIV's "scattered throughout" refers to the "Diaspora" (*Second Testament*). This term can refer to those living outside the Land of Israel, to those who, because of persecution, have been chased and have fled (Acts 8:1), or it can become a metaphor for those who choose to live in their homeland in a new social community. Shively Smith's research on diaspora living deserves quotation. She perceives Peter's "diaspora" as a voluntary choice rather than forced exile.

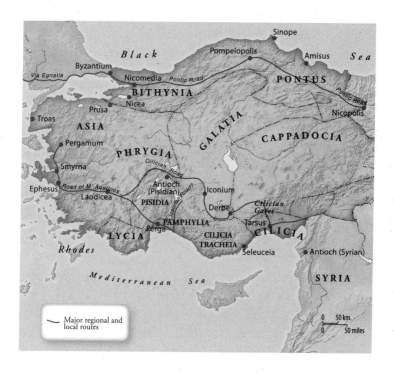

Diaspora Christians are a newly constituted people living as foreigners and strangers in their ancestral homeland or place of residence. Its configuration suggests that the diaspora experience does not always require a community's physical movement and resettlement. Diaspora does not indicate God's people leaving a place to which they hope to return. (Shively, *Strangers to Family*, 25)

Whether or not the exiles and temporary residents who make up the audience of 1 Peter have moved from one location to another, and I think that should remain a serious possibility, Smith has this one firmly in her grip: their existence is a diaspora existence. She continues with clarity about diaspora existence:

> First Peter, therefore, recreates the whole diaspora situation. It asserts that diaspora should be embraced, rather than remedied. In this epistle, the image of diaspora is not one of judgment, condemnation, and negative consequences. Diaspora is also not a potential avenue for avoiding persecution, suffering, and censure. Here, diaspora fosters a collective sense of belonging and obedience that persists. (26)

Diaspora then needs to be perceived as more than geographical migration. If there was a migration, however, these believers learned to live as a family, as God's household, in a location that did not welcome them.

The spiritual *and* social conditions of the believers addressed by Peter are sketched in "deceptively compact statements": they are known to God, which is the direct implication of "according to the foreknowledge of God the Father" (1:2; quoting Green, *1 Peter*, 14). God's redemptive work in claiming them for himself occurred "through the sanctifying work of the Spirit" (1:2), the aim of which is so the exiles and temporary residents could become "obedient to Jesus" through the consecrating, purifying power of being "sprinkled with his blood" (1:2; cf. Exodus 24). Add these three and you get **Father, Son,** and **Spirit,** but also **salvation, sanctification,** and **purification**—both triads will be needed for the exiles and temporary residents to live in the way of Jesus in their various locations across Asia Minor.

Peter's "grace and peace is yours in abundance" should not be minimized into a simplistic opening greeting—a Jewish version of "Hello" or "Greetings." But we should also be careful not to overinterpret either grace or peace. Rather, the goodness of God in redeeming people into this wonderful new community can become the space of peace for these exiles and temporary residents. It's their home away from home, their home until they return or until the Lord's return. Ellen Davis, in a sermon she preached in Nashville a decade back, puts a finishing touch on today's reflection:

> While striving for superficial forms of community will leave us lonely and undisciplined, a full recognition that we are in some way marginalized, alienated, and reeling from loss can propel us into the real community called "church." As we share in God's holiness, we may recognize each other as gifts of grace, and discover in the light of this grace that we have finally found our true home. (Davis, *Preaching the Luminous Word*, 306)

QUESTIONS FOR REFLECTION AND APPLICATION

1. What do you think of the suggestion that Peter's audience is or at least contains gentiles?

2. What does "election" mean to Peter?

3. How does diaspora living help foster community?

4. Have you ever experienced a church community that felt like home to you? What factors helped create that sense?

5. Shively Smith defines diaspora Christians as people living in a land as foreigners. In what ways is that true of how you live your Christian life in your country?

FOR FURTHER READING

Ellen Davis, *Preaching the Luminous Word: Biblical Sermons and Homiletical Essays* (with Austin McIver Dennis; Grand Rapids: Wm. B. Eerdmans, 2016).

SALVATION AS BIOGRAPHY

1 Peter 1:3–12

[3] *Praise be to the God and Father of our Lord Jesus Christ! In his great mercy he has given us new birth into a living hope through the resurrection of Jesus Christ from the dead,* [4] *and into an inheritance that can never perish, spoil or fade. This inheritance is kept in heaven for you,* [5] *who through faith are shielded by God's power until the coming of the salvation that is ready to be revealed in the last time.* [6] *In all this you greatly rejoice, though now for a little while you may have had to suffer grief in all kinds of trials.* [7] *These have come so that the proven genuineness of your faith—of greater worth than gold, which perishes even though refined by fire—may result in praise, glory and honor when Jesus Christ is revealed.* [8] *Though you have not seen him, you love him; and even though you do not see him now, you believe in him and are filled with an inexpressible and glorious joy,* [9] *for you are receiving the end result of your faith, the salvation of your souls.*

[10] *Concerning this salvation, the prophets, who spoke of the grace that was to come to you, searched intently and with the greatest care,* [11] *trying to find out the time and circumstances to which the Spirit of Christ in them was pointing when he predicted the sufferings of the Messiah and the glories that would follow.* [12] *It was*

revealed to them that they were not serving themselves but you, when they spoke of the things that have now been told you by those who have preached the gospel to you by the Holy Spirit sent from heaven. Even angels long to look into these things.

The Christian life is a biography. More than a birth, more than a childhood, more than an adolescence, and more than an adulthood. A biography describes a different story for each of us. Some of us get started earlier than others, most have some highs and lows, but each of us has a story to tell of God's love for us. Peter himself had a story to tell, and the New Testament describes enough incidents in his life to put together a mini biography.

One of Peter's favorite words points to big ideas for a new way of life, and that word is *salvation*. Peter's *theory* of salvation derives from his *biography* or *experience* of salvation. Let's look at how the New Testament describes salvation. In the sweep of the Bible, and especially from the Gospels on into the earliest churches, salvation was not reducible to a one-time moment. As in, "I got saved when I was twelve when I prayed the Sinner's Prayer." Or, as in, "I was saved when I was baptized." In the Gospels, where the verb *sōzō* occurs nearly fifty times, salvation is holistic: physical, spiritual, social, relational. Peter likes the noun *sōtēria*, "salvation," and it occurs twice in our passage (1:5, 9) as well as at 2:2 and 3:15. The verb occurs at 3:21 and 4:18. But the idea of salvation cannot be reduced to one word.

A theological and Christian life mistake is made when salvation is turned into a one-and-done event, or into one word and that word alone (like justification or forgiveness). Salvation is a lifelong experience. Peter would never have reduced salvation to his special moment of salvation. Another mistake is to make salvation entirely an individual affair. It's not. Paul, not Peter, says all creation groans for that great day of redemption (Romans 8:18–22). Peter would have agreed with Paul about that.

Read today's passage above again and mark each word connected to salvation. Notice these words as you read the passage: mercy, new birth, living hope grounded (!) in the resurrection of Jesus, inheritance, God's power, praise, glory, honor, end result, and the gospel. Add to these the acts of God the Father, the redemption of the Son, and the purifying work of the Spirit. Our passage is so replete with the ideas of salvation that one has to pause over each verse to get even a weak grip on the vastness of redemption. The Christian life for Peter has a biography: that life begins at, is sustained by, and will result in salvation. Put in other terms, it has a past, a present, and a future. It is unfortunate, then, that so many reduce salvation to a person's moment of salvation in the past.

A word from experience: as one person's biography differs from another's, so one person's spiritual story will differ from others. Too often churches have created the habit of similarity when it comes to conversion stories. That is, at times one gets the suspicion that everyone has to have an experience like Paul's or Martin Luther's. But no two stories are alike. God works in a variety of ways. Some people have a dramatic experience, some don't. Some get baptized as infants and grow into their faith in a way they can never remember not believing. Others get saved and then get baptized, and they can date it on a calendar and celebrate it annually. Yes, there is a past, but there is also a present and a future salvation.

SALVATION'S PAST

In the past the prophets studied and deliberated continuously over scriptures to discern the "time and circumstances" that the Spirit prompted in them about the coming of God's Messiah (1:10–11). A good example can be found in Daniel's ninth chapter. They learned, perhaps in disappointment, the Savior Messiah's coming would not occur in their time but in the future (1:12). One suggestion of experts about the prophets deserves to be given some attention. What were the prophets looking for in the scriptures? Peter says they were exploring "this salvation" (1:10). In what sense? Some have suggested the prophets were exploring the inclusion of gentiles, and this can be supported because of Peter's emphasis on the shift from we/us in verses three and four to "you" in verses five through twelve, if not to the end of the letter. I don't know about you, but I like this suggestion.

In an even deeper past God acted "in his great mercy" to reveal these ideas to the prophets that burst forth in the sending of his Son, who gave to the believers of this letter "new birth" (1:3). Here Peter at least echoes a marvelous set of verses in the prophet Ezekiel (36:25–27). The new birth leads to three prepositions: "into" hope, "into" an inheritance, and "into" salvation (1:3, 4, 5). What is remarkable in our passage is that our inheritance in the future fullness of the kingdom "is kept in heaven for" us (1:4). This could be translated "having been kept" (*Second Testament*). Either way, our future inheritance has been set for us in the past by God's election, has been and is now being preserved for us, and will be protected until the day we inherit it! So magnificent is this salvation that the angels "long to look into these things" (1:12).

We know about Peter's past from Mark's first chapter. He was a fisherman; he had a brother named Andrew. Peter was an observant Jew, and we know this because in Acts 10 Peter protested to the Lord himself when he was ordered to "kill and eat" food deemed unclean in the law of Moses. Peter's protest is "Surely not, Lord! . . . I have never eaten anything unclean" (Acts 10:13, 14). Then he met Jesus on the shore.

SALVATION'S PRESENT

Our own experiences of salvation, which for some happen over time and for others in a sudden moment, come to the surface often in today's passage. You might want to mark them in your Bible. It begins on the note of "new birth," which means God gave to us a new life or gave life to us again (1 Peter 1:3). Correct that: at verse twelve we learn it actually began with those who "preached the gospel to [us] by the Holy Spirit" (1:12). That's not enough for Peter, so hold on: we hang on to salvation now "through faith" as we "are shielded" by nothing less than "God's power," and that salvation "is ready to be revealed" as we walk by faith (1:5). That's all in just one verse. I have to add what Fleming Rutledge once said about faith in an Easter sermon she preached: "Being a believer is not a matter of accepting data; it is an attitude, a stance of the whole person yielding himself [or herself] in trust to the One who gives faith, who confirms faith, who brings faith to completion" (Rutledge, *The Bible and the New York Times*, 142). Walking by this faith-attitude and faith-stance in the present involves rejoicing amidst suffering with "grief in all kinds of trials" (1:6), and this suffering tests us and establishes the "genuineness of your faith" (1:7). That test shapes us to become people who love Jesus, who believe in Jesus, and who are "filled with an inexpressible and glorious joy" (1:8). Notice what verse nine says: we are *in the here and now* "receiving the end result of [our] faith, the salvation of our souls" (1:9). The future becomes present in the experience of the faithful follower of Jesus. Peter does not reduce salvation to something we received but expands it to something we are receiving. In chapter three, Peter will say that "baptism now saves you" (3:21). He's messing with some of our simplicities.

Luke's Gospel describes Peter's moment of salvation. He's on the shore. Jesus is, too. Crowds press around them, so Jesus gets into the boat with Peter, and from the boat Jesus teaches the crowds. When done he asks Peter to move to deeper water and lower his nets. Peter opines that he has done that all night with nothing to show for his labor. Peter does it anyway and catches such a great haul of fish that he needs others to help them bring the fish to shore. The whole event was numinous and luminous for Peter: he encountered God in Jesus, and he perceived Jesus for who he was. Peter admits his sinfulness, and Jesus matches that confession with a mission for Peter: he will become a fisher of humans (*Second Testament*, Luke 5:1–11). We can add to this the number of events in Peter's life when he experienced the glories of Jesus, when he struggled to comprehend Jesus, when he confessed Jesus as Messiah and also later denied Jesus, when he experienced grace and forgiveness from Jesus, and when he received the fresh winds of the Spirit at Pentecost—and then and there began to realize the significance of becoming a fisher of humans. He had years of deepening redemptive moments.

SALVATION'S FUTURE

One does not raise eyebrows by mentioning the past or the present of salvation. But when one suggests salvation is in our future, or not complete until the future, some may wonder if they've got enough to last or if they can lose it. Peter loves the idea of living now in the hope of future salvation. Notice, again reading through today's text, these future themes of salvation: salvation is a "living hope" (1 Peter 1:3), something that is "coming" and yet also ready but not yet "revealed" but will be "in the last time" (1:5). This future salvation occurs "when Jesus Christ is revealed" (1:7). In chapter two Peter says they are to crave "pure spiritual milk" so they can mature into their "salvation" (2:2), in chapter three that the present patience of the Lord awaits future "hope" (3:15), and in chapter four Peter writes that it is "hard for the righteous to be saved," an indicator of future redemption (4:18).

Fred Craddock reads today's passage through one word, *inheritance*. The idea is that we have an inheritance. He describes folks gathered with a legal authority to hear a will being read, wondering and anticipating and even fearing to hear what they would or would not inherit. The sermon he preached on this makes a very important point: our inheritance is guarded by God and our name will be heard, and after our name is heard, we will hear from God, "Here, this is yours." I take encouragement from Craddock's sermon (Craddock, *Collected Sermons*, 274–79).

It is Peter, above all writers in the New Testament, who connects salvation so tightly to the future. Peter knew salvation in the present, and he knew the testing of his faith well, but he must have been one who so looked forward to resuming fellowship and friendship with Jesus that he shifted the emphasis of salvation from the past and present to the future. Which is why Peter's first expression in today's passage is "Praise God!" His praise or blessing of God consumes three verses as Peter's prayer of praise morphs from one element of salvation to another. Peter's word behind the English word "Praise" is *eulogētos*, which derives from "saying a good word." So, let's together say a good word to God for the glories of salvation.

Questions for Reflection and Application

1. What is the difference between seeing salvation as a one-time event versus as an ongoing, lifelong experience? What are the practical implications of those differences?

2. How would you summarize each phase of the past, present, and future of salvation?

3. To study more about salvation in the Gospels, consider what one is saved from in the following passages: Matthew 1:21; 27:49; Mark 3:4; 10:52; Luke 7:50; 8:36, 50; 9:24; 17:19; 18:26, 42; 19:10; John 3:17; 10:9; 12:27, 47. What do you find?

4. Read Ezekiel 36:25–27 and draw parallels to 1 Peter 1:2 and 1:3, as well as 1:13–21. What stands out to you?

5. What is your own salvation biography? How does it connect with your life story?

FOR FURTHER READING

Fred Craddock, *The Collected Sermons of Fred B. Craddock* (Louisville: Westminster John Knox, 2010).

Fleming Rutledge, *The Bible and the New York Times* (Grand Rapids: Wm. B. Eerdmans, 1998).

THE THREE FACES
OF HOLINESS

1 Peter 1:13–2:3

13 Therefore, with minds that are alert and fully sober, set your hope on the grace to be brought to you when Jesus Christ is revealed at his coming. 14 As obedient children, do not conform to the evil desires you had when you lived in ignorance. 15 But just as he who called you is holy, so be holy in all you do; 16 for it is written: "Be holy, because I am holy."

17 Since you call on a Father who judges each person's work impartially, live out your time as foreigners here in reverent fear. 18 For you know that it was not with perishable things such as silver or gold that you were redeemed from the empty way of life handed down to you from your ancestors, 19 but with the precious blood of Christ, a lamb without blemish or defect. 20 He was chosen before the creation of the world, but was revealed in these last times for your sake. 21 Through him you believe in God, who raised him from the dead and glorified him, and so your faith and hope are in God.

22 Now that you have purified yourselves by obeying the truth so that you have sincere love for each other, love one another deeply, from the heart. 23 For you have been born again, not of perishable seed, but of imperishable, through the living and enduring word of God.

²⁴ *For,*

> *"All people are like grass,*
> *and all their glory is like the flowers of the field;*
> *the grass withers and the flowers fall,*
> ²⁵ *but the word of the Lord endures forever."*

And this is the word that was preached to you.
¹ *Therefore, rid yourselves of all malice and all deceit, hypocrisy, envy, and slander of every kind.* ² *Like newborn babies, crave pure spiritual milk, so that by it you may grow up in your salvation,* ³ *now that you have tasted that the Lord is good.*

Did you grow up in a church that sang these words? (I did. Every Sunday, if you care to know.)

> *Holy, holy, holy!*
> *Lord God Almighty*
> *Early in the morning*
> *Our song shall rise to Thee*
> *Holy, holy, holy!*
> *Merciful and mighty*
> *God in three persons*
> *Blessed Trinity!*

I vividly recall the low and high voices in our church in deep resonance and harmony. A reverence shaped the mood as we sang Reginald Heber's much-loved song. That word "holy" was sacred, the kind of word that could stop you in your tracks. And if it didn't, you were surely in need of repenting or reforming, or probably both. I did not know the meaning of "holy" when we sang it, but I felt something I could call "holy." What did I feel? Reverence. Awe. Pay attention. Seriously. Many too easily explain the word "holy" as separation, but that's only half or less of its meaning. The fundamental idea of holy or holiness is, first, this: God is holy, and holiness belongs exclusively to God and to God's presence. That's why Peter quotes an Old Testament anchor verse: "Be holy, because I am holy" (1:16; from Leviticus 11:44, 45; 19:2). To "be holy" means to be devoted to the God who is holy. So, second and third: those devoted to God are fit for God's presence, and in entering into God's presence they separate themselves from the world. So, God and God's presence, devotion, and separation. In that order. Those devoted to God must turn their backs on sin and worldliness. To begin at the end, with separation, gets it backwards in more than one way. To begin at the end turns holiness into a negative idea, and it also begins with our experience instead of who God is. God is holy; anything in God's presence must be devoted to God and fit for God's presence; and anything devoted to God must be removed from the common, the profane, and the sinful. One, two, three. Only that order explains what holiness means in the Bible.

> One: God alone is holy (presence)
> Two: Devotion to God means commitment to holiness
>   (devotion)
> Three: Devotion to God requires turning from sin
>   (separation)

Peter has just sketched a biography of salvation in 1:3–12. He now turns to a core theme for how the Christians of Asia Minor need to live if they are going to be faithful in the empire. That theme is holiness, and we will look at today's passage through the lens of holiness. The central instruction, "so be holy," is found in verses fifteen and sixteen in today's passage, but Peter turns this term over and over and each time a fresh term becomes visible: set your hope, do not conform, live . . . in reverent fear, obey the truth, sincerely love, rid yourselves, and crave pure spiritual milk. Holiness, like wisdom, appears with many faces on the stage of life. But we can only see the many faces of holiness if we remember the "one, two, three" above. When the moment is right, the right face appears. Some of the faces are positive, the devotion theme in set your hope, love, crave; and others are the negative, the separation theme, seen in do not conform, live in reverent fear, rid yourselves. We begin, as holiness itself does, with the positive theme of devotion to God, but with the reminder that the negative is the inevitable result of the positive. The one devoted to God turns toward God and, in doing so, turns from the negatives.

Holiness has fallen on hard times today. The lack of calls to holiness is not heard because many of us grew up in a kind of Christian fundamentalism that was too much "don't do" (negative) and not enough "do good, do justice, do love, do peace" (positive). Obsessions with micro-ethics—you can name the ones in your world—turned many toward a freedom, and at times the kind of freedom that had no limits. Such a way of life was and is not in line with the apostle Peter's teaching in this letter. We would all do well both to listen to him, and to strive to recapture a healthy, wholesome understanding of holiness. But holiness is not a "rules 'n regs" legalism, and holiness is not fundamentally negative. There is a balance to be discovered between leave-me-alone freedom and fundamentalist legalism's obsessions with the negative side of holiness. Without the one and two, every three leads astray.

THE FACE OF DEVOTION

Peter dashes in from the angels aching to look into redemption (1:10–12) to an image in 1:13 that nearly all translations cover with a more English-y expression. Behind "with minds that are alert" Peter wrote, literally, "surrounding your mental waist [with your robe]" (1:13; *Second Testament*). The image is a cloak or robe or tunic being pulled up from the bottom and tucked into the person's waist-belt or even wrapped around one's waist. This gave the legs room to move. Peter added to that image a term connected to sobriety. But both tucking in and sobriety are aimed at the redemption of "minds." That is, the exiles and temporary residents need a clear-headed, clear-thinking approach to life. That life can be reset if they "set [their] hope on" the grace that completes our salvation when Jesus returns (1:13). The image, when the pieces are glued together, inspires a mentally alert working life. Paul Achtemeier, who wrote an intense academic commentary on 1 Peter, jumped out from behind a rostrum to announce that "Drunken people in long garments are not very good at hard labor" (Achtemeier, *1 Peter*, 118). Notice, Peter believes one's hope in the return of Christ resets a person's life toward holiness. While many have turned the Second Coming into speculation, a genuine grasp of the Second Coming does not lead to speculation: it leads to living now in a way that is holy, that is devoted to the ways of God, to justice, to right-eousness, and to love. Holiness involves clear, sound thinking leading to the two and three of holiness.

A second face of devotion in today's passage appears down in verse twenty-two. Peter begins with their past salvation, "Now that you have purified yourselves," and that happens for the believer "by obeying the truth." Faith and obedi-ence merge here into a single response to the grace of God in Christ: the believer's faith is obedience to the truth. But notice something here: the NIV's "purified" translates a verb that could be translated "holy-fied" (Greek, *hagnizō*). That is, they have been made holy. Because they have been made holy, another face of holiness appears: the art of Christian love. He calls it "unmasked sibling-love" (*Second Testament*) or "sincere love" for one's siblings in Christ (1:22). The word used for love here is *philadelphia*, which broken into part means "love for one's siblings." Holy-fied people have the capacity to love sincerely, or without hypocrisy, feigned, pretended love. To love is to live in an affective commitment with another person, and that involves spending time with them and growing with them into Christlikeness. Easier to describe than do. Peter knows the challenges of loving Christian siblings, so he clarifies such love with the splendid little term "stretchingly," which is my more graphic translation of the term (*Second Testament*; the NIV has "deeply"). Holy-fied pops up again with his next expression: they have unmasked, stretched love because they do so "from *clean* hearts."

Notice how anchored Christian behaviors are in salvation. Salvation makes us fit for God's holy presence and empowers us for devotion to God. Peter's battery of instructions is preceded by the grace and power of God at work in us. The God who will judge them "impartially" (1:17) and lead them into the kingdom of God, the new heavens and the new earth, is the God who saved them. Peter tells us how God's salvation happened: "with the precious blood of Christ, a lamb without blemish or defect" (*Second Testament*, Hebrews 9:12, 14). Jesus lived our life, he died our death, and he was raised for our resurrection into the presence of God for eternity. Paul's letter to the Romans, especially chapter three, has attracted all the attention on how God redeemed us, but today's passage deserves some attention too. So central is Christ to salvation, Peter tells them Jesus was appointed by the Father before creation and just recently "revealed . . . for your sake" (sounds a bit like 1 Peter 1:10–12). As Catherine González reminds us, "We need to remember that what they are called to be [the faces of holiness] is totally based on what God has already done for them" (González, *1 Peter*, 32).

And we are not done with salvation at verse twenty-two: "For you have been born again" (1:23). The devotion theme of holiness flows from the salvation work of Father, Son, and Spirit, and a means of that work is the "living and enduring word of God" (1:23–24). You and I can be forgiven if we think this refers to our Bibles. It does, but only indirectly. Peter makes it clear he's referring to the gospel preaching they heard and responded to when he finishes off our chapter one with "this is the word that was preached to you" (1:24). Herein is a lesson for all of us: your Bible and mine resulted from gospel preaching. Maybe we should not be saying that we preach the Word of God (Bible), but that the Bible preaches the gospel to us!

Which is why Peter calls on the believers of Asia Minor to "crave pure spiritual milk" (2:2). The NIV's "spiritual" prevents us from seeing the connection of four terms: "word" (*logos*) and "word" (*rēma*) and "word" (*rēma*) and "spiritual" (*logikos*) in 1:23, 25 twice, and 2:2. To make this connection clearer I prefer "word-shaped milk" for 2:2 (*Second Testament*). Peter's idea of the gospel-word reveals another element of what salvation means and how it occurs. Those who crave this word-shaped milk will be nourished and will thus "grow into [a more complete, present] salvation" (2:2). As I have often stated in this *Everyday Bible Study* series, the gospel is first and foremost a message *about Jesus Christ* and only secondly a message of salvation for us. The gospel sermons of Peter in Acts (2, 3, 4, 10–11) were sermons about Jesus, and those who experienced that gospel were the ones who came to know that "the Lord is gracious" (2:3; *Second Testament*; NIV has "good").

This theme of devotion, which is the second face of holiness, elicits from us a desire to approach God, to worship God, to know the goodness of God, to obey God, to love God—and to love others straight from one heart to another.

Devotion to God establishes direction for us. As we move into God's presence, we turn our backs on sin, Satan, and systemic evil and injustice. This is the face of separation, the third face of holiness.

THE FACE OF SEPARATION

Holiness is about God, about God's presence, about what is devoted to God, and about separation from the common and profane. Which is why when Peter is about to instruct the believers to be holy in 1:15–16, he calls them to be "obedient children" who "do not conform" to their pre-salvation days (1:14). In today's passage we are introduced to three negative requirements and each of those requirements reveals what the past of these believers were like (1:14, 17–18; 2:1). The three negatives are "do not conform" and "live out your time as foreigners here in reverent fear" and "rid yourselves." Synthesized this means, *As you devote yourself to God's presence, flee from evil, sin, and systemic injustices.* These were the sins of the past for these exiles and temporary residents. This gives us insight into their pre-Jesus lives. They were marked by (1) "the evil desires you had when you lived in ignorance," (2) "the empty way of life handed down to you from your ancestors," and (3) "all malice and all deceit, hypocrisy, envy, and slander of every kind." If one has any questions about whether Peter's audience is Jewish or gentile, the answer is found in the first two expressions. They were gentiles. If you want more, read ahead at 1 Peter 4:3.

It has been said by experts that the two most concerning sins in the church planting work of the early apostles were immorality and idolatry. In our world, immorality is easier to spot than idolatry, but Kathleen Norris can help us spot the second term: "I no longer think idolatry is a problem of primitive people in a simpler time, those who worshipped golden calves in fertility rites. I have only to open a newspaper to contemplate the wondrously various way in which idolatry is alive in the here and now" (Norris, *Amazing Grace*, 92). A couple pages earlier she describes idolatry as the undoing of loving God, self, and others by exaggerating or obsessing over one or the others. If love is the center of life for God and for God's creation, then idolatry is distorted love becoming the god we worship. If Norris wrote that piece today, she would definitely include social media's temptation to promote ourselves, a promotion too easily generated by comparing ourselves to the self-presentation of others.

The not-conforming will evoke for many of us the same term in Romans 12:2. But instead of Paul's "the pattern of this world," Peter calls them not to be controlled by their former ignorant desires (cf. Acts 3:17). And even more, they had been liberated from their ancestral religious, social, ethical, political, familial, and cultural world. Sociologists call this "primary socialization," meaning the world into which we are nurtured by our families that was inscribed in our hearts and minds *reality itself*. If our family inscribed goodness, love, holiness, and justice, those were our reality. If our family inscribed hatred, disrespect, suppression of emotions, stealing, hypocrisy, and other toxicities, those toxicities became our reality. The believers to whom Peter writes learned idolatries, immoralities, desires, envies, hypocrisy, deceit, slanders, and ignorance. Their natural inclinations were to return to what ordered their world during the days of their primary socialization.

The good news was that salvation ushered them into a secondary socialization called holiness. For salvation-shaped-holiness to become their lived reality would require discipleship, and discipleship would require time to devote themselves more fully to the holy God and thus to separate themselves from the world's systemic grip. It required intentionally not conforming, living in reverent fear before God, and shedding like snakeskin the dysfunctional way of life they learned in their past, primary socialization. They were growing in a life that said "No" to a dysfunctional past, and they were learning to say "Yes" to the world God reveals in Jesus Christ.

QUESTIONS FOR REFLECTION AND APPLICATION

1. What does it change for you to think of holiness in terms of aspects one and two (God's presence and devotion to God) instead of just in terms of aspect three (separation from sin)?

2. How does holiness impact our ability to love in relationships?

3. For further study on the theme of judgment in 1 Peter see 1:7, 9, 17; 2:12, 23; 3:12; 4:5–6, 17–19. Record your observations.

4. What are the micro-ethics in your world? What are you told not to do in order to be holy?

5. How is the secondary socialization of discipleship helping you shed idolatry, immorality, and other inclinations as you move toward holiness?

FOR FURTHER READING

Paul Achtemeier, *1 Peter: A Commentary on First Peter* (Hermeneia; Minneapolis: Fortress, 1996). I found this quotation in Edwards, *1 Peter*, 55.
Reginald Heber, "Holy, Holy, Holy." Public domain. https://en.wikipedia.org/wiki/Holy,_Holy,_Holy! _Lord_God_Almighty#cite_note-Canterbury Hymnology-2.
Kathleen Norris, *Amazing Grace: A Vocabulary of Faith* (New York: Riverhead, 1998.

NAMING YOUR CHURCH

1 Peter 2:4–10

[4] As you come to him, the living Stone—rejected by humans but chosen by God and precious to him—[5] you also, like living stones, are being built into a spiritual house to be a holy priesthood, offering spiritual sacrifices acceptable to God through Jesus Christ.
   [6] For in Scripture it says:

> "See, I lay a stone in Zion,
>   a chosen and precious cornerstone,
> and the one who trusts in him
>   will never be put to shame."

[7] Now to you who believe, this stone is precious. But to those who do not believe,

> "The stone the builders rejected
>   has become the cornerstone,"

[8] and,

> "A stone that causes people to stumble
>   and a rock that makes them fall."

They stumble because they disobey the message—which is also what they were destined for.

⁹ But you are a chosen people, a royal priesthood, a holy nation, God's special possession, that you may declare the praises of him who called you out of darkness into his wonderful light. ¹⁰ Once you were not a people, but now you are the people of God; once you had not received mercy, but now you have received mercy.

To identify ourselves we name our churches. Church of the Holy Spirit. Church of the Redeemer. First Baptist Church. Joyful Noise Church. Living Stones Church. Epic Life Church. Cyber Sanctuary Church. St. Patrick's.* Almost no church has a sign out front with only "Church." When Kris and I were in Denmark I noticed that churches there don't have cool names. Most of them are Church of Denmark churches but even "Lutheran" (or its Danish equivalent) did not appear on signs. Their churches are parish churches with a name at times as old as the community, like Dragør Church in, you guessed it, Dragør. Most Americans want something more identifiable and now catchier and cooler. In the early 2000s, if my memory serves me right, many churches removed their heritage's denominational name, like Baptist, Lutheran, Roman Catholic, Presbyterian, etc., and renamed the church with something less traditional and to distance that church from the oddities and dysfunctions of the denomination. For example, the Baptist General Conference removed "Baptist" in 2008 and renamed themselves Converge Worldwide. (Neither catchy nor cool.) What I do know is that names matter. Today's passage assigns names to the church, and we can learn lots from the names Peter used.

---

* A site cataloging names, from which some of the above names are taken, is: https://www.nichepursuits.com/church-names/.

WHERE TO BEGIN?

Once we get to the last two verses of today's reading, we will be given a heady list of names for those who gather in Jesus' name, but before we get there, we have an observation to make: Peter begins today's reading with Jesus and hangs on to him for five verses. Naming a church begins with Jesus or it loses its way. Those in the church are those "who come to him" who is the "living Stone" (2:4). Here Peter may surprise you as much as he surprised the Christians of Asia Minor. The Jesus whom believers approach is a rejected-by-humans but chosen-by-God and honorable-to-God Stone.

The quotation of Isaiah 28:16 in verse six gave rise to the important terms in verses four and five. So, let's go to Isaiah 28:16. In that chapter Isaiah vehemently criticizes the leaders of Jerusalem for their toxicities and promises a coming stone in verse sixteen. That stone will "make justice the measuring line and righteousness the plumb line," and he will put all wrongs to the right (28:17). Bad shepherds leading Israel badly is a theme in the prophets, and God will resolve the bad shepherds by being the shepherd himself or by sending a good shepherd (see Ezekiel 34). Peter informs the believers that Jesus is that good shepherd, or to switch metaphors dramatically, that Stone.

But he was rejected by humans, and here he points his listeners back to the arrest, trial, and crucifixion of Jesus (Mark 14–15). Though rejected by humans, the Stone is both chosen and honorable to God. The NIV's "precious" translates a word commonly connected with public honor (*entimos*), so I have translated it "honorable" (*Second Testament*; 2:4, 6, 7). Noticeably, Peter says this three separate times. Yes, the origin is found in Isaiah 28, but Peter adds two more to the prophet's one. The image at work in both Isaiah and then for Peter is a construction crew leader evaluating and rejecting a stone as unfit, but then God coming along and choosing that very Stone as the "cornerstone," which shapes the entire edifice (2:7–8). Jesus is the Chosen Stone and the Honored Stone (above all other stones). Some, however, reject this Stone (*lithos*) and stumble on him. Those are the ones upon whom the Rock (*petra*) falls in judgment (2:8). Others believe in this Stone and find the salvation Peter emphasizes in chapter one.

We can draw this together: the Jesus to whom his followers come is a rejected-by-humans Jesus. He is not the way of power, success, wealth, popularity, fame, and glory. His social media didn't have an abundance of Likes. His is the way of the cross. But beyond that cross is Easter and the ascension. On the other side of the defeat of the cross is the victory of new life. The Jesus behind the names on the church needs to be *both* the rejected Stone and the honored Stone. The church is a place where the full depiction of Jesus needs to be proclaimed and displayed. Not just glory and good times, but suffering and bad times.

CHURCH NAMES

So, how does Peter describe those who come to the rejected-and-honored Stone? They are a "house" (2:5). Or, perhaps a household, the most common location of church gatherings in the first century. Yet, the context has so much temple language (priests, sacrifices) that temple is more like the image in mind. Plus, the temple can be called the "house" of God (Acts 2:2; 7:47–49). Exiles and temporary residents found the church-as-household image attractive, comforting, and identity-shaping. They found a new family. Again, Shively Smith describes their diaspora life: "diaspora comes about because people choose to embrace their identity as scattered yet related kinship groups, who exist on the fringes of their provincial neighborhoods" (Smith, *Strangers to Family*, 26). The church folks are both present and different. Their diaspora life then has a "double-consciousness" (Smith, 11).

Four doubled expressions now name the church, the household of those following Jesus: chosen people, a royal priesthood, a holy nation, God's special possession (2:9), interrupted in verse ten with a mission, and then resumed with two doubled expressions: not the people/now the people of God and no mercy/now receiving mercy. These church names echo three major Old Testament passages:

Chosen people: Isaiah 43:20–21
Royal priesthood: Exodus 19:5–6
Holy nation: Exodus 19:5–6, and Exodus 24.
God's special possession: Exodus 19:5–6 and
    Isaiah 43:20–21
Not people/now people: Hosea 2:23
No mercy/mercy: Hosea 2:23
    On Stone, see also Psalm 118:22 and Isaiah 8:14;
    also Matthew 21:42.

I'm not sure what you might see here, but reading each of these Old Testament passages in context will percolate into many insights. Peter depicts the church people of Jesus as those who have entered into the covenant God made with Israel. Israel's story becomes the church's story. The church has no story without Israel's story. Both Israel and church have no story without the Jesus story. Pheme Perkins rightly says that "the imagery [drawn from Israel's scriptures] . . . highlights the dignity of the community that is built on Christ" (Perkins, *First Peter*, 44).

In addition, these terms pertain to the whole church, and to each person as part of the family household. Notably, "priesthood" is not just for the pastor or priest; it is the mission and ministry of each believer. Each of these terms, then, reminds us of our collectivity and calling *as a community*, and our individual life fits into that collectivity. We can only be royalty and priestly because Jesus is the king and the great high priest. As those who believe in him, we enter into his royal rule and his priestly work.

Another observation: these terms are not triumphant and conquest terms. As if we can say "Hear hear, we are the one and only true people of God." No, each of these terms connects the church to Jesus, and the Jesus of this passage is the rejected-then-honored Stone. And connection to Jesus is connection to Israel and its story. So, it is an Israel's-rejected-honored-Jesus-shaped royal priesthood, etc. These names for the church shape the mission of the church to be a Jesus-the-Stone mission. And this means we need to turn now to the mission of the church as stated in this passage.

HOW TO LIVE AS THE CHURCH

If these names for the church are ours, then we hear our mission in three church mission elements. First, and this has already been discussed and was prompted in part by Isaiah 28, the church is composed of *believers* who embody believing in ongoing faithfulness (2:6, 7; see also 1:5, 7, 9, 21; 5:9). Second, the church has a *priestly, praying* mission. A royal kind of priesthood, mind you. Those who approach the Stone "as living stones, are being formed as a Spirit-shaped house into a devoted priesthood to offer Spirit-shaped sacrifices" that will have a "good acceptance by God," and this priestly mission and acceptance are "through Jesus Christ" (2:5; the first quotation from *The Second Testament*). As a prophet reveals something from God to the people of God, so the priest intercedes to God for the people of God. Stone-shaped churches name their priestly calling as they embody it in approaching God on behalf of the people of God, the community, the nation, and the world. That is, they pray.

Third, they are called to *declare a message about God*. Peter gives the communities of believers those six names listed above so "that [they] may declare the virtues of the one who called you out of darkness into his stunning light" (2:9; *Second Testament*). A very special word—drawn from discussions about ethics, morality, and especially public behavior—is at the heart of 2:9. The word is *aretē*, and a standard translation is "moral excellence" and "virtues." The church is called to declare the virtues of God—the goodnesses of God. It is to be a God-oriented community. Peter's term for the customary worshipful singing in Israel is *hallel*. *Hallel* refers to a song of praise and adoration, and to find such an ancient song, read Psalm 118 (or all of Psalms 113–118, called the Hallel). Yes, *hallel* is from *hallelujah*. These songs were sung as the people of God approached God in the temple. This reminds us of "as you come to him" in 1 Peter 2:4. The virtues of God in Psalm 118 include God's goodness, love, presence, helper, refuge, strength, salvation, and the one who does mighty things. Put biblically, the virtues of God emerge from the specific experiences of the people of God, and therefore are personal. The mission of declaration witnesses to the experiences of the people of God, and as Gardner Taylor once said, "There is no use theorizing about what God can do and cannot do with someone for whom the Lord has done great things." He continues with what God is able to do: "He can bring peace out of confusion, joy out of sorrow, victory out of defeat, day out of darkness, triumph out of tragedy, health out of sickness, sunshine out of the storm, spring out of winter, laughing out of weeping, and holiness out of sin" (Taylor, *Quintessential Classics*, 27). Instead of requiring the people of God to witness to someone else's attributes of God, let us

51

nurture the people to declare in their own words the God they have come to know.

What we name our church will always fall short of the mission of the church. What matters most are two themes: the church is a Jesus-the-Stone community, and the community's mission is to reflect Jesus-the-Stone in the wideness of its ministry as believers, priests, and God-praisers.

QUESTIONS FOR REFLECTION AND APPLICATION

1. Why do you think it's important to Peter to emphasize that Jesus was rejected by humans?

2. What is the importance of Jesus being chosen by God and precious?

3. How do the many Old Testament quotations function in this excerpt?

4. What is the name of your church, and what is the history and significance of that name?

5. In what ways do you see your Christian community living out the mission of the church according to Peter here? (Believers who are praying and declaring a message about God.)

FOR FURTHER READING

Gardner Taylor, *The Words of Gardner Taylor,*
   volume 3: Quintessential Classics, compiled by
   Edward L. Taylor; Valley Forge: Judson, 2000).

Special note to the reader: For the Bible study on 1 Peter 2:11–12, see p. 9.

A STRATEGY FOR THE POWERS

1 Peter 2:13–17

[13] *Submit yourselves for the Lord's sake to every human authority: whether to the emperor, as the supreme authority,* [14] *or to governors, who are sent by him to punish those who do wrong and to commend those who do right.* [15] *For it is God's will that by doing good you should silence the ignorant talk of foolish people.* [16] *Live as free people, but do not use your freedom as a cover-up for evil; live as God's slaves.* [17] *Show proper respect to everyone, love the family of believers, fear God, honor the emperor.*

What is recorded in today's reading is the result of apostles and pastors and deacons and prophets discerning how best to live as followers of Jesus in the Roman empire. They learned strategies that both preserved their status in society, which are often called "stations of life," and that gave them opportunities to make an impact for the good of the gospel. One strategy Peter must have learned from Jeremiah:

This is the text of the letter that the prophet Jeremiah sent from Jerusalem to the surviving elders among the exiles and to the priests, the prophets and all the other people Nebuchadnezzar had carried into exile from Jerusalem to Babylon. . . .

Build houses and settle down; plant gardens and eat what they produce. Marry and have sons and daughters; find wives for your sons and give your daughters in marriage, so that they too may have sons and daughters. Increase in number there; do not decrease. Also, seek the peace and prosperity of the city to which I have carried you into exile. Pray to the LORD for it, because if it prospers, you too will prosper. (*Second Testament*, Jeremiah 29:1, 5–7)

Israelites knew defeat, captivity, exile, but they also knew return. As they waited for the return to the Land, they accommodated and even assimilated to life in the diaspora. Life in diaspora without accommodations becomes unbearable. Jeremiah's fundamental vision was "seek the peace and the prosperity of the city" where they found themselves. Such a strategy, detailed by Peter at 2:11–12 (p. 9), is the opposite of rebelling and rioting. Most learn on Day One that rebellion leads to death and disaster. So, they learned survival strategies that enabled them to approximate the life they desired.

Today's reading is a strategy for a marginalized set of "exiles and temporary residents" who are themselves seeking the good of their society by doing good (2:11–12). Peter's strategy stands with Paul's in Romans 13:1–7 but very much contrasts with what we find in the book of Revelation and also forms tension with how Peter and other apostles behaved just after Pentecost (Acts 4:18–20). Different accommodations for different locations are the only way to explain these various responses to the powers. The governmental powers mentioned in 2:13–17 are the first of five "stations of life" addressed in 2:13–3:12. Similar assignments, though more restricted to the household, are found also in Colossians 3:18–4:1, Ephesians 5:21–6:9, and 1 Timothy 5:1–6:2. They address people according to their station in life, and they are not all the same. Once again, different accommodations for different locations.

BIG PICTURE

Peter gives no fewer than eight instructions, seven of them packed into the last two verses of our passage. Let's concentrate on the big picture instruction of 2:13: "Be ordered under every human-shaped creation [NIV has "human authority"; the Greek word is *ktisis*, a standard term for a creation]." He has in mind the cultural, human-developed forms of structure, system, power, and authority. He knows no system is perfect, but Peter also knows it's far wiser to avoid getting in trouble with the authorities. Civil disobedience was known in Peter's world, though the freedoms and rights today are vaster than they were in his world, especially for exiles and temporary residents. What might "be ordered under" or, as the NIV has it, "submit" have meant? Something easily missed needs to come into the light. There were no verse or paragraph divisions in the original letter of Peter. What precedes and follows Peter's "be ordered under" are instructions about doing good. Which means we can read verse twelve and hear that we are to do good, and then we can read verse fifteen and hear that we are to do good. Verse twelve and verse fifteen surround the call to submit in verses thirteen and fourteen. The implication, then, of ordering under is not "do whatever they tell you to do" or "be dominated by." Instead, it means to live within the system in manner of doing good for others. To be sure, the danger of the term found its way into colonialism, patriarchy, and domination. Even more, this term and especially 2:18–25 were used by New World Christian slaveowners to legitimate enslavement and abuse. That misappropriation deserves its presence and denunciation as we read this section of 1 Peter.

When he writes "for the Lord's sake" he gives agency to the believers to live an orderly, good life in accordance with this fresh experiment with a Christian strategy (2:13, 15, 17). Dennis Edwards is right: "The obedience that Christians have to the government is not so much an endorsement of the rulers of this age but an act of devotion to God" (Edwards, *1 Peter*, 105). By "ordering under" Peter means for the believers to live within the system without rebelling against the system (as with Jeremiah above). He mentions "emperor," and Nero is the emperor for those who date this letter in the early 60s. America, in spite of its routine rhetoric of how bad some president is, has never known someone remotely as corrupt as Nero. Oddly, it must be noted, Peter uses the term *basileus*, which could be translated "king," which in Latin is *rex*, which is the very term Rome despised for its emperor! He then turns to local provincial "governors." Their primary objectives were "controlling political volatility and protecting imperial interests" (Smith, *Strangers to Family*, 64). "Ordering under" imperial-appointed powers is my favored expression instead of "submit" since this latter term has gained too many accretions of physical and sexual abuse. Ordering under, or intentional, voluntary accommodation to the powers, again, is a strategy, an experiment, not a permanent always-live-like-this law. The emperor has "supreme authority," which in any reading about the emperors is a thin expression of how many of them lived. A good way to read about the emperor is to work one's way through Suetonius' *Lives of the Caesars*. Here are a few lines about Nero from his account:

> Punishment was inflicted on the Christians, a class of men given to a new and mischievous superstition. (*Nero*, 16)

> He castrated the boy Sporus and actually tried to make a woman of him; And he married him with all the usual ceremonies . . . and treated him as his wife . . . he even desired a sexual relationship with his own mother. (*Nero*, 28)

> . . . he resolved on the death of all the eminent men of the State . . . putting to death whomsoever he pleased on any pretext whatever . . . He boasted that no Prince had ever known what power he really had . . . (*Nero*, 36, 37)

This is but a taste of one of Rome's egomaniacal, vicious, immoral emperors.

The word Peter uses for the emperor was brief; for the governor we get an expansion: "who are sent by him to punish those who do wrong and to commend those who do right. For it is God's will that by doing good you should silence the ignorant talk of foolish people" (2:14–15). Notice how positive this expression is of the governor's relations with Christians— there is no official persecution of believers by the authorities (yet). Here again, the strategy is in full bloom: if they do good, that is work for the common good, they will be given "public praise" (*Second Testament*). The impact of a good person with a good life can squelch the opponents of the gospel who slander believers. It is hard to bad-mouth a person of good works like Mr. Rogers. The aim, again, is not to justify all powers but to exhort Christians not to engage in unjust actions.

The word *every* before human authority deserves a serious look. If every means always submitting to every human authority one encounters, then we have a recipe for abuse. Abuse is wrong. Always. Every time. And every authority who abuses—sexually, physically, relationally—is wrong. Peter cannot have meant every and always. Peter's strategy was issued with assumed limits and constraints. This very strategy Peter himself disobeyed in Acts 4:18–20. A good reminder comes from the African American woman scholar, Shively Smith, who warns us all about the dangers of the household regulation theme of ordering under. This set of instructions in 2:11–3:7 "is a stylized Greco-Roman household code that some later interpreters misused, misinterpreted, and misappropriated in order to underwrite power hierarchies between husbands and wives, masters and slaves, and state and citizens" (Smith, *Strangers to Family*, 70).

Think of what African Americans, Latinos and Latinas, Asian Americans, and Indigenous Americans experience when they hear "every" connected to the word "submit" when tied to political authorities in the USA. In the Civil Rights movement, leaders like Martin Luther King, Jr., lived within the system while opposing the system. Civil Rights advocacy for nonviolent resistance became an embodied resistance that helped transform the system and its powers. Abusive, authoritarian personalities and people with power look for angles and opportunities to abuse but also for structures and systems that mask and spiritually legitimate abuse. In her recent book Laura Anderson exposes the power abuses of "high control religions" (Anderson, *When Religion Hurts You*), and this is a book that needs to be read along with every discussion about authority, power, and submission—and ordering under. Peter's "every" does not mean an unconditional every.

SMALLER FOCUS

Now seven staccato-like instructions for how to accommodate oneself, or to order oneself inside human systems: live like you are liberated, which implies not exploiting your liberation (spiritual liberation is in mind since some were slaves); though liberated in one's public life, live as a "slave" to God; respect everyone; "love the siblingship" (*Second Testament*; NIV has "family"); live in awe before God; and finally back to the top of today's passage: "honor the emperor."

These six instructions fill in the blanks of the big picture that opens this passage and these six expand that big picture also. It expands by making the siblingship in Christ more vital than the empire's sense of family; by living as God's slaves (not Rome's, and the next passage will develop this); and by showing proper awe to God. All this permits the believers to live inside the system while not embracing the system as the one true life and worldview.

In the United States, we live in a democratic republic, which means the ordinary person has far more power than such a person did in the Roman empire. Our freedoms, Peter reminds them, ought not to be exploited. I give an example of at least taking too much advantage of if not exploitation of freedom by American evangelicals. When I began my academic career, an evangelical was someone who believed in the gospel of (personal) salvation and worked for the expansion of the gospel to others. Leading lights included John R.W. Stott and Billy Graham. In the 1970s through the 1980s American evangelicals became more and more politically involved, accomplishing some good and then gaining power with puffy chests. Then evangelicalism became bellicose. Taking back America for God ran right through the American evangelical scene.

By the 2000s, the word evangelical "became synonymous with 'conservative Christian,' and eventually with 'white conservative Republican' (Tim Alberta, *The Kingdom, the Power, and the Glory*, 11). The term evangelical has increasingly lost its religious connections, and recent studies have shown that evangelicals are more shaped by partisan politics than by the gospel itself! When "honor the emperor" usurps "fear God," the evangelical movement has not just lost its way; it has become idolatrous. A wonderful southern pastor, Nibs Stroupe, in speaking about the demonic powers of this world that seek our allegiance, preached these words, and they speak to the exploitation of freedoms too many American evangelicals have committed: "*These* are the demonic powers that this story is asking us to engage: the powers of this world which we have turned into idols, the idols which compete with God for the loyalty of our hearts. The powers that tell us that if we are not loyal to them, if we do not obey them, if we do not worship them, then our lives will fall apart and we will lose all meaning" (Stroupe, *Deeper Waters*, 11). When these exploitations and idolatries lead to Stroupe's more pointed criticisms—like racism, materialism, sexism, and homophobia—then we know it is time to repent.

QUESTIONS FOR REFLECTION AND APPLICATION

1. What is the difference between being dominated by ruling authorities and living well within an authoritarian system by doing good to others? What are some practical ways these two approaches could play out?

2. What is the value of "different accommodations for different locations" regarding Christian responses to secular powers? Compare Romans 13:1–7 and Acts 4:18–20 with today's passage.

3. What qualifications does Peter put on Christians' obligations to be "ordered under"? Do you think Christians are obligated to obey sinful, abusive authorities? Why or why not?

4. What does "evangelical" mean to you? Do you claim that label for yourself?

5. What are some survival strategies you use to approximate the life you desire when life isn't ideal? How can you live as well as possible right now?

FOR FURTHER READING

Tim Alberta, *The Kingdom, the Power, and the Glory: American Evangelicals in an Age of Extremism* (New York: Harper, 2023).

Laura E. Anderson, *When Religion Hurts You: Healing from Religious Trauma and the Impact of High-Control Religion* (Grand Rapids: Brazos, 2023).

Nibs Stroupe, *Deeper Waters: Sermons for a New Vision* (ed. Collin Cornell; Eugene, Oregon: Wipf & Stock, 2017).

Suetonius, "Nero" in *Lives of the Caesars*, 2 vols.; Loeb Classical Library (trans. J.C. Rolfe; Cambridge, Mass.: Harvard University Press, 1997), 2.82–179.

SLAVERY IS SLAVERY

1 Peter 2:18–25

¹⁸ *Slaves, in reverent fear of God submit yourselves to your masters, not only to those who are good and considerate, but also to those who are harsh.* ¹⁹ *For it is commendable if someone bears up under the pain of unjust suffering because they are conscious of God.* ²⁰ *But how is it to your credit if you receive a beating for doing wrong and endure it? But if you suffer for doing good and you endure it, this is commendable before God.* ²¹ *To this you were called, because Christ suffered for you, leaving you an example, that you should follow in his steps.*

> ²² *"He committed no sin,*
> *and no deceit was found in his mouth."*

²³ *When they hurled their insults at him, he did not retaliate; when he suffered, he made no threats. Instead, he entrusted himself to him who judges justly.* ²⁴ *"He himself bore our sins" in his body on the cross, so that we might die to sins and live for righteousness; "by his wounds you have been healed."* ²⁵ *For "you were like sheep going astray," but now you have returned to the Shepherd and Overseer of your souls.*

A Bible I often read as a college student because it was more literal than most, the American Standard Version of 1901 (ASV), translates the first word in today's passage with "Servants" (so does NASB, ESV). But in translating it with servant, however genteel, lies a million sins. The big one is the conceit that first century slavery was so much better than America's New World slavery or at least not nearly as awful as New World slavery. Since, it is supposed, the New World slavery was so awful compared to ancient Rome's slavery, the word "servant" is more appropriate. That view of ancient slavery was popular for decades, and a view I once held. The discomfort for Bible readers to see the word slave led to the use of the word servant. Wrong and wrong. The real improvement for accuracy's sake is the NIV's "slaves" (also NLT, NRSVue). The CEB has a fine nuance with "household slaves." We will say more below. Slavery is slavery, always, and a household slave remains a slave, a domestic slave. Servant softens the harshness of slavery's realities. Before we reflect briefly on today's passage together, I offer a brief sketch of some uncomfortable facts about slavery in the world of Peter, that is, in the Roman empire.

SLAVERY: SOME REALITIES

The best definition has been provided by an expert on slavery in the ancient world. Keith Bradley writes,

> Slavery by definition is a means of securing and maintaining an involuntary labour force by a group in society which monopolises political and economic power. (Bradley, *Slaves and Masters*, 18)

Slavery describes a perceived inferior human being under the total authority of another perceived superior human being, and the reality of that perception of inferiority is established by power and authority. The enslaved were branded, shackled, hands were cut off, legs were broken, castrated, and iron collars have been recovered witnessing to the cruelty of masters to the enslaved. They were cremated alive, crucified, and handed over to wild animals in the amphitheater. The bodies of the enslaved could tell the story of slavery better than the literary and archaeological record. Slaves could not marry in the technical sense because marriage implied ownership and inheritance. Male slaves never became "men" but were always "boys," a term used both to degrade and to lower these humans made in God's image in social status.

The most influential ancient writer about the philosophy of slavery was Aristotle. We read his account of slaves and slavery in his book *Politics.* He compared tools of *production* and tools of *action* and thus saw the enslaved as "an assistant in the class of instruments of action" (1.2.6). Of course, the relation of a master to one of his enslaved persons was asymmetrical: "whereas the master is merely the slave's master and does not belong to the slave, the slave is not merely the slave of the master but wholly belongs to the master" (1.2.6). The enslaved is "property" and thus "a human being belonging by nature not to himself but to another" (1.2.7). As in the sexes where the male is by nature designed to rule the female, so in slavery: there are some who are "by nature slaves" (1.2.13). Thus, "he is by nature a slave who is capable of belonging to another . . . and who participates in reason so far as to apprehend it but not to possess it" (1.2.13). Aristotle's analytics know no boundaries: "the usefulness of slaves diverges little from that of animals" (1.2.14). For Aristotle "slavery is an institution both expedient and just" (1.2.15). What Aristotle wrote was one important chapter in the "bible" for slavery in the New World.

Something we need to face together and in discussion: the instructions by both Paul and Peter for the enslaved to act in obedience to their masters may well have come from their new theological orientation, but the impact of their teachings would have kept the enslaved in their place, would have led to more of the same, and would have made abolition unimaginable. The apostles never denounced slavery as an immorality of the age. While many today want to think Paul's ultimate aim with Philemon was to have Onesimus emancipated, the earliest Christians certainly did not read him that way. The archbishop of Constantinople, St. John Chrysostom, in what is called the "Argument" to his sermons on Philemon, more than three centuries after Paul wrote the letter, said this:

> . . . that we ought not to withdraw slaves from the service of their masters. For if Paul, who had such confidence in Philemon, was unwilling to detain Onesimus, so useful and serviceable to minister to himself, without the consent of his master, much less ought we so to act. For if the servant is so excellent, he ought by all means to continue in that service, and to acknowledge the authority of his master, that he may be the occasion of benefit to all in that house. Why dost thou take the candle from the candlestick to place it in the bushel?

Another church father from the fourth century, Cyprian, in an address *Address to Demetrianius* (8), seems to have at least probed the immorality of slavery in these words to a Christian slaveowner:

> From your slave you yourself require service; and though a man, you compel your fellow-man to submit, and to be obedient to you; and although you share the same lot in respect of being born, the same condition in respect of dying; although you have like bodily substance and a common order of souls, and although you come into

this world of ours and depart from it after a time with equal rights, and by the same law; yet, unless you are served by him according to your pleasure, unless you are obeyed by him in conformity to your will, you, as an imperious and excessive exactor of his service, flog and scourge him: you afflict and torture him with hunger, with thirst and nakedness, and even frequently with the sword and with imprisonment. And, wretch that you are, do you not acknowledge the Lord your God while you yourself are thus exercising lordship?

The contradiction between someone who is a "fellow-man" and an enslaved person who could be flogged and scourged and deprived of food and water and clothing only reveals how invisible the immorality was to nearly all of the Christians until after the Enlightenment. May God pierce us. May we repent. May we turn to Scriptures all over again to see the truth.

SERIOUS STUDIES OF SLAVERY

Keith R. Bradley, *Slaves and Masters in the Roman Empire: A Study in Social Control* (New York: Oxford University Press, 1987).

Keith R. Bradley, *Slavery and Society at Rome*, Key Themes in Ancient History (Cambridge, MA: Cambridge University Press, 1994).

Jennifer A. Glancy, *Slavery in Early Christianity* (Minneapolis, MN: Fortress, 2006).

Thomas Wiedemann, ed., *Greek and Roman Slavery*, rev. ed., Routledge Sourcebooks for the Ancient World (New York: Routledge, 1989).

Even if you need to take a break from slavery's realities as I had to do when I studied slavery intensively nearly a decade ago, only by digesting this (very) brief sketch of some facts about slavery can we begin to understand the message of Peter in today's passage. Where to begin? Perhaps the wisest is to locate ourselves in Peter's world and to assume Peter, his many readers, and especially the slaves *had but two options:* endure slavery or rebel against slavery. Since the latter was sure death, the former is how slaves and their advocates learned to live. This letter was written to provide wisdom for believers in Asia Minor to negotiate life in the Roman empire in a way that sustained faithfulness. Peter's words to the enslaved are shaped by the same concern, and we perhaps need to be reminded of the nature of this letter, which was a "writing from the underclass for the underclass, not the overlord" (Smith, *Strangers to Family,* 165).

HE RECOGNIZES BRUTALITY

The term Peter first uses is *oiketēs,* slaves who worked inside the household (cooking, serving, managing, etc.). They were "domestics" (*Second Testament*). But domestics were slaves because they were owned, exploited bodies, and Peter exhorts them to submit or live inside the slavery system both to the "good and considerate" as well as to the "harsh." Such submission must not be seen as passivity, but somehow as doing good. Which means, they were to submit to God and then to the master. Such a way of life could express agency by the slave, and for Peter "peaceful submission" could then be "evidence of genuine Christian faith" (Edwards, *1 Peter,* 116).

Because he can do very little about first century Rome-based slavery, Peter only acknowledges the brutality of masters. The words used do not indicate the depth to which some masters sunk, but the words do speak: "masters" trans-literated is *despotēs*, from which the English pejorative despot derives; "harsh" could be translated as "rascals" or even "jerks." Other terms expressing the tough existence for the enslaved include "pain" and "unjust suffering" and "beating" (2:18, 19, 20). When read in the context discussion above, these terms evoke abuses well-known to the enslaved inside the master's household. Let's hope the slaveowner, or master, described by Peter, was not a Christian.

In this instruction to slaves, Peter expresses his strategy of doing good for the common good (see 2:11–12 at p. 9). When one can do nothing about it, such a strategy may be the only option. When one *can* do something about it, resistance and dissidence are options. It is fatal, as well as morally unconscionable, for church leaders and pastors to advise enduring abuse today. Not only do we have rights and duties, but we are increasingly creating safeguards, policies, and advocacy groups.

Shively Smith's Witness to Peter's Strategies

My truth rings clear this moment. As much as I am a daughter of those who fought and declared openly their full humanity and rights as God's creation, I am also the daughter of those who made an honest assessment of their odds and decided it was more expedient in the moment for them to survive the ungodly, inhumane, and evil systems forced on them. I am as much the daughter of those who survived the middle passage and auction blocks as I am the daughter of those who fought for civil rights and continue to fight for equal access and fair treatment for all in the current movements of Black Lives Matter and others. Many of us are indebted to both decision makers: those who confronted evil disparities as well as those who concealed their critique in the mask of social compliance, cultural performance, and verbal niceties so that their progeny could live to fight another day. Therefore, here we are, continuing this dance between hidden and public resistance or affirmation. Some of us are the product of both choices—to survive and to challenge in varying degrees and at different moments as strangers and family, whose plights are linked one to the other. (Smith, *Strangers to Family*, 169)

HE PROVIDES TWO NEW FRAMES

In the strategy to make an impact in the community as well as save their skin, Peter reframes slavery in two different ways. First frame: their ordering under is not because (1) the master is lord, (2) slavery is right, or (3) Rome is God's world power. Their behaviors are to be done "in reverent fear of God" (NIV) or "in all awe" before God (*Second Testament*). Down in verse twenty, Peter says doing good and suffering for it is "commendable before God." If the domestic slave thought hard about this they would realize, along with those addressed by Paul (Colossians 3:22–4:1), they were being challenged to reframe their life in the system as an act of love and service to God, *and not to their masters*. Their actions then would be acts of resistance while conforming to social expectations. Some call this kind of strategy foot-dragging. Call it justice-making, too. Pheme Perkins puts an exclamation on the internal resistance at work in Peter's instructions when she writes, "Christ did not heal the flock in order to sacrifice the sheep" (Perkins, *First and Second Peter*, 54).

What Peter develops with full force is a second frame: the domestic slave's approach to the seemingly inevitable mistreatment and abuse by rascally masters could be reframed as participating with Christ in his sufferings (2:21–25). Peter frames it like this: first, he says it is their calling as Stone-followers (2:4–9). Second, he sees an "example" in Christ's own life (2:21), and the term he uses here is used for the wax tablet on which the teacher wrote letters for children to trace so they could learn the art of writing letters. Third, he switches images from the wax tablet to footprints: "that you should follow in his steps" (2:21). Fourth, he details the suffering of Jesus in quoting from Isaiah 53:4, 5, 6, 9 in today's passage (1 Peter 2:22, 24–25). Using Isaiah, he states particulars with "insults" and "sufferings" (2:23). Fifth, he observes how Christ responded to abuse with what he did not do: "he did not retaliate" and "he made no threats," and what he did do: "he entrusted himself to him who judges justly" (2:23; see Matthew 5:38–44). In other words, exactly what he just told the domestics in 2:18 and 2:20.

These two frames ought to lead us to a particular view of God. Namely, that God is on the side of the oppressed, that God sees and hears and knows the sufferers. Jesus has been there; Jesus reveals God in the fullness of what makes God God. Therefore, God is with the sufferers and is oppressed *as one of them*. The older line of "preferential option for the poor" that has risen from the prophets of Israel can be expanded to a preferential option for the enslaved.

Peter wanders off topic—like a typical preacher—when he shifts from Christ as example for the sufferers to Christ as Savior, who "'himself bore our sins' in his body on the cross." He did this, and here he sounds much like Paul in

Romans 6, so they/we could die to the sins of retaliation and making threats and live in a way that does what is right at the right time (2:24). That is, his "wounds" become our healing. Peter backs up to the past of these gentile believers by closing down today's reading when he describes their *past* as wandering like lost sheep but their *present* as having "returned to the Shepherd and Mentor of your selves" (2:25; *Second Testament*).

HE GIVES THREE
PRACTICAL STEPS

The context is unjust suffering by the domestic slaves. Peter reframes their behaviors as a life before God and one that participates in Christ's sufferings. He weaves into those two themes three practical steps for the believers. First, they are to "submit," *but only indirectly,* to the slave masters by ordering their lives under God (2:18). We cannot emphasize this indirection enough. Yes, at the quotidian level they remained slaves, but in their hearts and minds they were ordering their lives under God and under God alone. Second, they were to do good (2:20). Remember this is the theme of 2:11–12 and doing good appears often in this letter (see 2:14, 15, 20; 3:6, 17; 4:19). Doing good could be a broad sweep of being nice and doing good things, but I explained previously (p. 9) that this term is best explained as participating for the common good. Which for the domestics would have meant the master's household's productions, which then gave slaves the opportunity to frame their labor as a contribution to the community. Third, they were to "follow in his steps," and here again Peter sounds like Paul (1 Corinthians 11:1). A domestic slave who had given her life to Jesus was to map her life on the paradigm of paradigms: the life of Christ. So far, we can say Jesus is the Stone, the Savior, and the Shepherd (parallel to Mentor). Jesus' life was the map they were to use for the journey. That map was one of trusting God, looking to God in the midst of suffering, and non-violent resistance rather than retaliation.

Sometimes theologians call this cruciformity and other times Christoformity and at other times Christlikeness. Some of those theologians, in my own hearing, have been down on the formerly popular (for youth) WWJD bracelets, but the theologians were mistaken. I know from both experience working with college students and in my own family that such a bracelet functioned for the wearer as a witness to others that he or she wanted to be seen as a follower of Jesus. Like wearing a cross or getting a Christian tattoo. What some perceive as superficial self-promotion the wearer may well see as learning to "follow in his steps." I'm inclined to say, *leave such persons alone.*

Let us close this reflection down by pondering with Dietrich Bonhoeffer the power of our participating in the sufferings of Christ, first with a short statement of his and then with a longer one:

> Suffering willingly endured is stronger than evil; it is the death of evil.
>
> Even though Jesus Christ has already accomplished all the vicarious suffering necessary for our redemption, his sufferings in this world are not finished yet. In his grace, he has left something unfinished . . . in his suffering, which his church-community is to complete in this last period before his second coming. This suffering will benefit the body of Christ, the church. Whether this suffering of Christians also has power to atone for sin (1 Peter 4:1) remains an open question. What is clear, however, is that those suffering in the power of the body

of Christ suffer in a vicariously representative [German, *stellvertretend*] action "for" the church-community, "for" the body of Christ. They are permitted to bear what others are spared. (*Discipleship*, 134, 222)

That second statement of his could make some nervous but think of it this way: those who suffer for Christ benefit those who don't suffer. They suffer to the benefit of others. Think of it this way, too: suffering embodies a witness to the gospel unlike no other witness and has the power to go deeper than words.

I conclude this reflection on a difficult text by repeating an observation above: in this passage Peter has nothing to say to the slaveowners, the masters. Unlike Ephesians 6:9 and Colossians 4:1, Peter provides no instructions to the slave's superior. We don't know why, but we can speculate that it could be because there were none in Peter's churches. Or perhaps the slave demographic was so numerous that words for the masters were unnecessary. His silence is an eloquence.

QUESTIONS FOR REFLECTION AND APPLICATION

1. How do the realities of American slavery compare with ancient slavery?

2. How have Peter's (and Paul's) writings been used to prop up institutions of slavery throughout history and even today?

3. When you consider the context that slaves in Peter's day had only two options (endure slavery or rebel and probably be killed), how does that influence your understanding of Peter's instructions to slaves?

4. How is your context different from Peter's? What should your perspective and action be toward slavery, oppression, and abuses today?

5. How does "doing good" for you differ from how Peter encouraged his recipients to do good?

FOR FURTHER READING

Aristotle, *Politics* (Loeb; translated H. Rackham; New Haven: Harvard University Press, 1932).

Dietrich Bonhoeffer, *Discipleship* (Dietrich Bonhoeffer Works 4; Minneapolis: Fortress, 2001).

John Chrysostom, *Homilies on Philemon*, at https://www.newadvent.org/fathers/23090.htm

More: Cyprian, *To Demetrian* 8 (trans. Coxe, *Ancient Nicene Fathers* 5:459–60)

EVANGELIZING THE OTHER HALF

1 Peter 3:1–7

¹ Wives, in the same way submit yourselves to your own husbands so that, if any of them do not believe the word, they may be won over without words by the behavior of their wives, ² when they see the purity and reverence of your lives. ³ Your beauty should not come from outward adornment, such as elaborate hairstyles and the wearing of gold jewelry or fine clothes. ⁴ Rather, it should be that of your inner self, the unfading beauty of a gentle and quiet spirit, which is of great worth in God's sight. ⁵ For this is the way the holy women of the past who put their hope in God used to adorn themselves. They submitted themselves to their own husbands, ⁶ like Sarah, who obeyed Abraham and called him her lord. You are her daughters if you do what is right and do not give way to fear.

⁷ Husbands, in the same way be considerate as you live with your wives, and treat them with respect as the weaker partner and as heirs with you of the gracious gift of life, so that nothing will hinder your prayers.

Peter has a strategy in his instructions to persons in various stations in life. Put simply, by doing good, a Christian has the opportunity both to protect the church and *affect* the world by tossing light in dark places. Peter believes these followers of Jesus can impact the powers of government as well as the masters of slaves. In today's passage, he informs a married woman that her way of life can lead her unbelieving other half to the truth about Jesus Christ. Husbands, who get far less attention here, probably because there were fewer of them, are instructed to treat their wives honorably and so lead both into a deeper spiritual life. Marriage, which Edith Wharton in her novel *The Age of Innocence*, called a "miracle of fire and ice," has always had its challenges and glories (Wharton, 7).

Once again, and I will say this more than once, what Peter says to wives here is a *strategy* sent to various churches *in that time* because they were experimenting with how best as Christians *to live in the Roman empire*. These are not timeless, context-less rules for marriage. These verses are his strategy for that time. We can learn from him without turning his statements into laws. Recall that the first century Roman world was shaped by status, and people knew their location or station in life, which is exactly why Peter addresses women according to their social status location. People knew where they fit, and they conducted themselves according to that location. Ordinaries deferred to the powers; slaves to their masters; wives to their husbands. Times have changed, and we'll get to that below.

WIVES AND HUSBANDS

The verb is often translated "submit" (NIV, CEB) though the NRSVue oddly joins hands with the ESV by softening it to "be subject." The NLT ramps up the NIV with an egregious exaggeration: "you must accept the authority of your husbands." Each of these translations reflects the hierarchical, patriarchal social context of the first century. Each of these also runs the risk of generating abuse of women by authoritarian men. The Greek term behind these translations is *hypotassō*, and that term derives from the cultural, customary ordering of society. Peter's strategy, as we have already seen with respect to government and slavery, is to *use the social order for the sake of goodness*. Today we don't believe in slavery, and we are grateful the social order has changed. Nor do we have an emperor and neither do we think the president of the USA is the "supreme authority" in a nation that believes in "We, the people." Nor, then, do we need to think the first century's hierarchical, patriarchal pattern needs to be resurrected or lived into today. These last three sentences flow out of the italicized words just before them.

Peter urges the wives to make use of the culture's structure *in order to convert their husbands to the faith*. He is not teaching some God-given hierarchical family order. As Catherine González has written, "the word to these wives is to try to show their husbands that by being Christians they have become better wives, more loving, less demanding for expensive clothing and jewelry" (González, *1 Peter*, 81). The apostle does not assume all the husbands are unbelievers (cf. 3:7), but the emphasis is on how wives can impact their husbands *by doing good*. Recall the theme of 2:11–12 and its practices at 2:14, 15, 20; 3:17; 4:19. The "doing good" manifestations for wives with unbelieving husbands include "without words," "by the behavior of their wives" (3:1), the "beauty" of virtue surpasses the beauty of the body, "the inner self," and the enduring impact of "a gentle and quiet spirit" (3:2–4). Their model is formed by the "holy women of the past" like Sarah who submitted to her husband, Abraham, when she called him her "lord" (3:6). This is found in Genesis 18:12. Finally, goodness is seen when these women "do what is right and do not give way to fear" (3:6). There is much of value in Peter's instructions for today, but I say so as a man who listens to women. Wives with unbelieving husbands today know the impact of their embodied witness; they too affirm the superiority of inner over external beauty when it comes to influencing husbands in the direction of faith; and women today continue to draw strength from women in the Bible, whether it is Sarah or Miriam or Deborah or Ruth or Esther or Huldah or Mary or Philip's daughters or Junia or Priscilla.

Our generation knows the potential danger of authoritarian husbands, whether they are non-Christian or claim to be Christian, taking advantage of the language of submission in order to dominate and abuse their wives into doing what the man wants, disrespecting agency, and thereby damaging and even traumatizing the woman. The gentle arts of relationships should never violate or eliminate the will of the wife. It must be observed, then, that "ordering under" can be an evangelistic tool OR it can be a weapon of domination. The character of the man will often determine which it is, which is why Peter's next verse turns to the man's virtues.

In their famous book, *Boundaries*, Henry Cloud and John Townsend wrote something three decades ago that is as true today as it was then: "We have never seen a 'submission problem' that did not have a controlling husband at its root" (Cloud and Townsend, *Boundaries*, 164). Character is what matters most. Which is why we can turn to the wry, piercing comment made of Lord Peter Wimsey in Dorothy Sayers' wonderful novel about Oxford University, *Gaudy Night*. The challenge was for the man to be truly egalitarian, which in the novel he clearly could not be. So, the narrator writes, "To take such a line and stick to it, he would have to be, not a man but a miracle" (Sayers, *Gaudy Night*, 222).

As an egalitarian, I ask to continue with a couple more thoughts. The rise of complementarianism, which seems to have been kicked off in the 1970s with Marabel Morgan's *The Total Woman* and the conservative Christian male reaction against the Equal Rights Amendment, has created a culture in American evangelicalism that at times makes complementarianism a theological platform alongside the (far more important) classic doctrines of the faith. That culture found its organization in the Council for Biblical Manhood and Womanhood. Then The Gospel Coalition, a gathering of (nearly entirely) evangelical males, connected gospel, orthodoxy, and complementarianism on its platform. However one explains the rise, many pastors, authors, and leaders believe complementarianism is the Bible's way.

Complementarianism is not a first century reality, though it has some connections to the first century. Rather, today's complementarians are post-1950s black-and-white TV evening, family sitcom, post WWII ideals, and all with the smell of pioneer America's idealized, romanticized family structures. When Margaret Atwood looked back to that era, she wrote, "In the 1950s, women were informed in numerous ways that their role was now to be a supporting one. They were to ditch their wartime Rosie the Riveter overalls and their independent incomes, act helpless and cute like Lucille Ball, and fulfill their femininity through having children, renouncing thought, and deferring to their husbands. Men who did not want to be Type A hyper-achievers were failed men, and women who did want that were failed women" (Atwood, *Burning Questions*, 399).

That Peter's instructions to women in today's reading were designed as a strategy for believing women with unbelieving husbands to win them to Christ, and not some eternally fixed structure for marriages of all times in all places kicks complementarianism in the shins. Having said that, Peter's words carry deep meaning for wives with unbelieving husbands today. A second, harder kick in the shins is that Peter's world and our world are completely different. If the fundamental idea was for the wives *to use their cultural system to win one's spouse*, a different cultural system (like twenty-first century America) presents considerably different instructions. To order oneself under the order of the modern world is to order oneself in a much more egalitarian, equalitarian society and marital relationship. Marriage in our society, as Catherine González cleverly terms it, is not a "corporation" but a "cooperative" (González, *1 Peter*, 82). Instead of calling one's husband "lord," our world urges women to call their husband "honey." Instead of appealing to the acts of submission in the holy women of old, a modern society appeals to the agency and leadership of women in the early church.

Peter's words to wives urges them to ask, how do we best live in the twenty-first century in a way that is faithful to the gospel and in a way that maximizes our impact for Christ? Look to Beth Moore, to Katya Covrett, to Jamie Clark-Soles, to Lynn Cohick, to Karen Swallow Prior. In various ways these women, like the holy women of the past, are exercising their gifts for the good of the gospel.

Women throughout history have fought against patriarchal authority in the ways available to them. Peter gave women some ways to do good and possibly influence the men around them toward goodness in his culture. Consider the words of Margaret Atwood for a way women can fight patriarchy today.

The #MeToo moment is a symptom of a broken legal system. All too frequently, women and other sexual-abuse

complainants couldn't get a fair hearing through institutions - including corporate structures - so they used
a new tool: the Internet. Stars fell from the skies. This
has been very effective and has been seen as a massive
wake-up call. But what next? The legal system can be
fixed, or our society could dispose of it. Institutions,
corporations, and workplaces can houseclean, or they
can expect more stars to fall, and also a lot of asteroids.
(Margaret Atwood, *Burning Questions*, 338)

HUSBANDS AND WIVES

Doing good for the husband looks like this: "be considerate" and "treat them with respect" (3:7). Once again, Peter's
words emerge out of a hierarchical, patriarchal social culture
in which women were considered inferior to men. If some
Greek philosophers were followed, women were incomplete
males and therefore inferior. In a near contemporary Jewish
text to 1 Peter, the *Letter of Aristeas* reaches some sad depths
in its estimate of women: "'How can one reach agreement
with a woman?' 'By recognizing,' he replied, 'that the female
sex is bold, positively active for something which it desires,
easily liable to change its mind because of poor reasoning
powers, and of naturally weak constitution. It is necessary
to have dealings with them in a sound way, avoiding provo-
cation which may lead to a quarrel. Life prospers when the
helmsman knows the goal to which he must make the passage" (§ 250–251; *Old Testament Pseudepigrapha*, volume 2;
trans. R.J.H. Shutt). It would not be inaccurate to think that
perhaps Peter, but surely many in the ancient world, would
side with this understanding of women. Peter wants Christian
husbands to break free from that ancient cultural mindset.

Noticeably, Peter's words order the husbands *not to treat women with authority and power and domination,* but with love, grace, respect, and Christian virtues. They are to "honor" their wives (*Second Testament*), which means holding them up for glory and praise by others.

They are—deep inside—to perceive their wives as "co-heirs of life's grace" (*Second Testament*), and this can only mean as spiritual equals. Peter undermines the asymmetry of Greco-Roman husband-wife relations. In its place, he offers an equalization that over time would yield egalitarian relations. This spiritual- and relational-equality comes to expression when husbands and wives pray together. When that relationship is as God designed it, Peter suggests their prayers would not be "cut off" (*Second Testament,* 3:7). His image is one's prayers fizzling out before reaching the ears of the Lord.

QUESTIONS FOR REFLECTION AND APPLICATION

1. In what ways does the context of these churches shape the way Peter advises them?

2. Does what Peter wrote in 3:1–6 sound like a man's view of how wives should behave? What might it sound like if a woman rewrote those verses?

3. Compare what is said to women in 3:16 with what is said to all believers in 3:13–16. What are your observations? How similar are the two passages?

4. What has been the effect on women today concerning ideals of body size and shape as well as the right clothing? How can Peter's words speak to that issue?

5. How do Peter's words in this section counter the prevailing treatment of husbands toward wives in his day? How could they improve husbands' actions today?

FOR FURTHER READING

Margaret Atwood, *Burning Questions: Essays and Occasional Pieces, 2004 to 2021* (New York: Doubleday, 2022).

James H. Charlesworth, ed., *The Old Testament Pseudepigrapha*, volume 2 (Garden City: Doubleday, 1985). I became aware of this text in reading Perkins, *1 Peter*, 59.

Henry Cloud and John Townsend, *Boundaries Updated and Expanded Edition: When to Say Yes, How to Say No To Take Control of Your Life* (Grand Rapids: Zondervan, 2017, 1992).

Dorothy Sayers, *Gaudy Night* (London: Victor Gollancz, 1949).

Edith Wharton, *The Age of Innocence* (Everyman's Library 202; New York: A.A. Knopf, 1993).

EVERYBODY

1 Peter 3:8–12

[8] *Finally, all of you, be like-minded, be sympathetic, love one another, be compassionate and humble.* [9] *Do not repay evil with evil or insult with insult. On the contrary, repay evil with blessing, because to this you were called so that you may inherit a blessing.* [10] *For,*

> *"Whoever would love life*
>   *and see good days*
> *must keep their tongue from evil*
>   *and their lips from deceitful speech.*
> [11] *They must turn from evil and do good;*
>   *they must seek peace and pursue it.*
> [12] *For the eyes of the Lord are on the righteous*
>   *and his ears are attentive to their prayer,*
> *but the face of the Lord is against those who do evil.*

Peter's instructions for the various persons in various stations of life moved from the powers (2:13–17), to domestic slaves (2:18–25), to wives (3:1–6), and to husbands

(3:7). His final instruction concerns "all of you" (3:8), a kind of summary listing of what it means to do good in a diaspora life as believers. He addresses how the believers are to relate to one another (3:8), how to relate to unbelievers (3:9), which leads to a lengthy citation of Psalm 34:12–16 (1 Peter 3:10–12).

RELATIONS WITH ONE ANOTHER

Since Peter sorts things in Peter's way, he deserves attention for the groups he has listed: the governmental powers clearly pertain to the relations with the public, but the slaves, wives, and husbands pertain to relations with one another in the family of faith. Two features stand out for me: first, the "all" means the slaves and siblings with the wives and husbands; and second, the absence of fathers and children, which appear in other household regulations. I don't know why the absence, as it is very unlikely these husbands and wives were not parents with children. One can suggest these groups were those that were most in need of instruction. We add in passing that in chapter five Peter will address the elder-younger folks, but elders are not identical with parents, and younger persons aren't the same as children.

Community entails unity, and genuine unity creates community. We all need it, especially when we are down and out or exiled or suffering or in the diaspora. For a church or a group of Jesus-followers to have "unity of mind" never has been achieved if it means agreeing on everything. Coerced belief is not unity of mind. Oneness of mind for a group means believing the essential gospel along with a commitment to a gospel-shaped life, which for Peter is a salvation that leads to holiness (1:3–2:3). They can all learn to be "sympathetic," that is, to acquire the virtue of becoming aware of another person's pain.

"Sibling-love" (*Second Testament*) raises to the surface what underlies both the first two relations as well as the next two, namely, the family relationship that comes from union with Christ. In the New Testament the church is a family of siblings, with very little emphasis given to the need for either fathers or mothers. This once again emphasizes the equality of believers.

The NIV's "tender heart" could be translated "good empathies," since the Greek word combines "good" (*eu*) with "empathies" (*splanchnoi*). The idea of good intensifies the virtue of being an empathic person, or the capacity to feel what others feel vicariously, without sliding into smushing one another's integrity and difference. It takes imagination to be sympathetic, the result of which is an ability to think with and like another person. Empathic persons enter into the feelings of others for the sake of support, relief, and healing. This term, along with *sympathetic*, describes the way of Jesus who observed the pain and suffering of others, who entered into that pain to feel with them, and then did what he could to alleviate their suffering (cf. Mark 1:41; 6:34). The disciples and the authors of the Gospel knew Jesus as a man of empathy and sympathy.

The NIV's "humble mind" can be shifted helpfully to "impoverished." If one recognizes how important social status, or honor and shame, was in the world of Peter, then this term refers to those who know their location, live in that location, but also live faithful to the ways of Christ. I think of Anna and Simeon in Luke's second chapter, the two senior citizens who longed for the days of redemption. I think, too, of the famous passage in Philippians 2, with words like these: "in humility value others above yourselves, not looking to your own interests but each of you to the interests of others" (2:3–4). Such a view of the term in 1 Peter strikes the note deftly because such self-understanding yields the unity and sympathy and empathy and sibling-love Peter inscribes.

These virtues, when practiced well, will result in the public's seeing them as doers of good, and the public will witness a way of life that stands in contrast to the way of the Roman empire. The church is an alternative community, one that not only seals itself from the empire but that subverts the way of the empire by its way of life.

RELATIONS WITH THE PUBLIC

In the passage that follows today's reading we will encounter the very issue that gives rise to what Peter writes in 3:9–12: namely, suffering at the hands of others for any number of reasons, some of them persecution for the faith. Peter instructs what he heard from Jesus: no retaliation (Matthew 5:38–42). In fact, just like Jesus, too, active resistance is urged by going the extra mile. For Peter that means bless those who do evil to shame them from their unjust actions. Kindness, goodness, and grace often form the spiritual weapon that demolishes evil and injustice. We have already quoted a line from Bonhoeffer in discussing 2:18–25, but now we include what he said before it: "Instead, by suffering, the disciple will bring evil to its end and thus will overcome the evil person. Suffering willingly endured is stronger than evil; it is the death of evil" (Bonhoeffer, *Discipleship*, 134). Jesus' words, like Peter's, formed a strategy for dealing with Rome. Peter has updated a Christian ethic but only by riffing on the words of his Lord.

Peter knows from Scripture, Psalm 34:12–16, that a blessing is promised to those who walk in the way of God when the surrounding world is opposed. Good speech, the pursuit of good and avoidance of evil, and the pursuit of peace are all strategies for living in an empire with the hope of both survival and impact. The worldview of the Psalmist is Peter's: God knows, God sees, and God will reward those who do his will. These are good, good words when doing good seems hopelessly useless. Perhaps you noticed that Psalm 34:17 ends with the promise that God hears "their prayer" and that it ties back to the husband and wife's prayers being heard (1 Peter 3:7). That's an ultimate good.

QUESTIONS FOR REFLECTION AND APPLICATION

1. Why does Peter choose the particular groups he addresses regarding stations of life in this part of his letter?

2. What does Peter's use of sibling language like "brotherly love" say about the kinds of relationships he expects in the churches?

3. How does a tender-hearted disposition, or good empathies, help create supportive relationships among believers?

4. How does doing good as a strategy disrupt life as usual in the Roman Empire?

5. In what ways could you demolish evil and injustice in your culture by living out kindness, goodness, and grace?

FOR FURTHER READING

Dietrich Bonhoeffer, *Discipleship* (Dietrich Bonhoeffer Works 4; Minneapolis: Fortress, 2001).

SUFFERING AND CHRIST

1 Peter 3:13–22

13 Who is going to harm you if you are eager to do good? 14 But even if you should suffer for what is right, you are blessed. "Do not fear their threats; do not be frightened." 15 But in your hearts revere Christ as Lord. Always be prepared to give an answer to everyone who asks you to give the reason for the hope that you have. But do this with gentleness and respect, 16 keeping a clear conscience, so that those who speak maliciously against your good behavior in Christ may be ashamed of their slander. 17 For it is better, if it is God's will, to suffer for doing good than for doing evil. 18 For Christ also suffered once for sins, the righteous for the unrighteous, to bring you to God. He was put to death in the body but made alive in the Spirit. 19 After being made alive, he went and made proclamation to the imprisoned spirits—20 to those who were disobedient long ago when God waited patiently in the days of Noah while the ark was being built. In it only a few people, eight in all, were saved through water, 21 and this water symbolizes baptism that now saves you also—not the removal of dirt from the body but the pledge of a clear

*conscience toward God. It saves you by the resurrection of Jesus
Christ, [22] who has gone into heaven and is at God's right hand—
with angels, authorities and powers in submission to him.*

Most agree that at the time this letter was written
there was no official, Rome-initiated persecution of
Christians because they were Christians. Opposition to
the gospel may not have been official but it can be said it
was, at least at times, officially ignored when it happened.
Suffering runs front to back in this letter, as can be seen
in 1:6; 2:18–25; 3:13–17; 4:1–6, 12–19; 5:8–10. The experience was characteristic of Israel's captivities and exiles, in the
opposition to and crucifixion of Jesus, and in the mistreatment of the earliest apostles by the authorities in Jerusalem.
Paul's own catalogue of suffering in 2 Corinthians 11:16–33
could illustrate the sorts of abuse the Christians addressed by
Peter had endured and would continue to experience.

SUFFERING

Peter often uses general terms, like "trials" (1:6) and "suffering" (2:19–21, 23; 3:14, 17, 18; 4:1, 15, 19; 5:10). You might
wonder what the particulars were. Adding to the "beatings"
inflicted upon slaves (2:20), today's reading opens a window on more specifics: verbal insults, slander, and threats
(3:14, 16). More than the behind-closed-doors gossip, what
Peter has in mind are verbal scaremongering, insinuating bad
motives for good behaviors, and unjust accusations that harm
reputation and personal peace. It appears that the Christians
in Asia Minor were beginning to experience widespread
opposition for their faith, and, at the time of this letter, a
primary form of opposition was verbal smear campaigns,
character assassinations, defamations, social lowering, and
belittlements. Gossips carried the smears from house to

house. It is some comfort to observe that Peter is not accusing fellow Christians of doing this to one another. Peter's advice is entirely directed at believers responding to those who oppose the gospel.

RESPONSE

How to respond? Everyone has a double instinct when experiencing character assassinations and status lowering: first, to defend oneself; second, to attack back. Listening in order to learn how one was wrong, of course, is excluded when the attacks are truly unjust. What to do when the defamations are unjust? Peter's first word, very common in this letter, is *to keep on doing good* (2:14, 15, 20; 3:6, 17; 4:19). Which means doing what is "right" (3:14), what is compassionate, what is merciful, what is loving, what is honoring. Over and over the Bible urges the kind word to the harsh accusation, but it does this not to tolerate abuse or injustice but as a strategy for survival and impact—with the hope (3:15) that justice will re-form the system.

Second, they are not to "be scared of their scare nor be agitated" (3:14; *Second Testament*). Peter is not prohibiting anxiety or emotions that accompany the body's created instinct to protect itself from what it recognizes as danger. Rather, Peter has his eye already on 3:18's paradigm: the lot of the faithful follower of Jesus in the first century was at times physical suffering as a witness to Jesus Christ. It would have been normal for hands to sweat when facing some bully. That's not Peter's concern. He wants them to face the trial as faithful participants in the way of the cross. Which is exactly why, third, Peter says "in your hearts revere Christ as Lord," or to make their devotion Christ as Lord and Christ alone (3:15). The Stone, the Savior, the Suffering Servant—that's the Christ to whom they are to devote their life. They were to muster the courage to identify with Jesus and his followers publicly.

Fourth, their courageous faith needs intellectual preparation too: "Always be prepared to give an answer" (3:15), or a "defense" (*Second Testament*). The word evokes being called into the dock or to be challenged on the spot to provide a reasonable answer for what one believes. Apologetics operates best when a person's life embodies consistency with the gospel. Consistency gives the response an integrity that can strike the conscience and heart of the accuser. First century questions revolved around claims that Jesus was the Messiah: *Was he not crucified? How is a crucified Galilean the Jewish Messiah?* That he was raised: *If raised, where is he? The dead are not raised.* And that the Christians were not good Romans or Bithynians: *Look at our good behaviors. At our good relations. At our actions for the common good.* Peter learned in those early days after Pentecost the need to defend the faith and how best to do it. Here is Peter in action:

> The apostles were brought in and made to appear before the Sanhedrin to be questioned by the high priest. "We gave you strict orders not to teach in this name," he said. "Yet you have filled Jerusalem with your teaching and are determined to make us guilty of this man's blood."
>
> Peter and the other apostles replied: "We must obey God rather than human beings! The God of our ancestors raised Jesus from the dead—whom you killed by hanging him on a cross. God exalted him to his own right hand as Prince and Savior that he might bring Israel to repentance and forgive their sins. We are witnesses of these things, and so is the Holy Spirit, whom God has given to those who obey him." (Acts 5:27–32)

97

I like Dennis Edwards' imaginative sketch of how this all worked out for believers: "The Christian community eagerly performs good works, which may invite hurtful words (and possibly actions) by hostile onlookers, accompanied by questions about why the Christians behave as they do (4:4), followed in turn by a respectful apologetic offered by the Christian believers. What comes after may very well be regret on the part of the accusers" (Edwards, *1 Peter*, 153). And I like the short story sketch of Leo Tolstoy. Simon, a husband, like so many characters in Tolstoy's fiction, is poor, who struggles a bit with alcohol and putting food on the table and adequate warm clothing on his wife, goes to the village to collect debts from his previous labor. The hoped-for debtors promise to pay him later. On the way home, having spent what he had on vodka, Simon passes by a naked man at a shrine and walks on. Then thinks better of Christian duties. He returns to the man, covers him with his own coat, and takes him home to a very upset wife, Matryóna. Simon describes the circumstances to his wife:

> As I came to the shrine I saw him sitting all naked and frozen. It isn't quite the weather to sit about naked! God sent me to him, or he would have perished. What was I to do? How do we know what may have happened to him? So I took him, clothed him, and brought him along. Don't be so angry Matryóna. It is a sin. Remember, we all must die one day.

The short story continues with her responses, which evolve:

> Angry words rose to Matryóna's lips, but she looked at the stranger and was silent.
> Simon said: "Matryóna, have you no love of God?"

Matryona heard these words, and as she looked at the stranger, suddenly her heart softened towards him. She came back from the door, and going to the oven she got out the supper. Setting a cup on the table, she poured out some kvas. Then she brought out the last piece of bread and set out a knife and spoons.

As they ate, she was moved more.

And Matryóna was touched with pity for the stranger and began to feel fond of him. And at once the stranger's face lit up; His brows were no longer bent, he raised his eyes and smiled at Matryóna. (Tolstoy, "What Men Live By," 764)

His short story moves faster than either his novellas or (endless) novels, but the evolution of Matryóna's response describes the sort of reality doing good can accomplish to those who are neglected, rejected, or in opposition. Goodness is the Christian's best apologetic.

Apologists tend toward liking challenges and debating the challenges. Losing can be a nightmare for the apologist. There is a long-in-tooth discussion whether or not C.S. Lewis laid down his apologetics mantle after his evening knock-about with Professor Elizabeth Anscombe. He most likely did (McGrath, C.S. Lewis, 250–57). What is not long-in-tooth is that Lewis, so far as I know, did not lash out against her. He had learned, however humbling it may have been (if it was), the strategy of Peter: do your defense "with meekness and awe" (3:15; Second Testament) so you can walk about with a "clear conscience" (3:16). These are the cushions, the padding, moments of doing good, the rhetorically artful response that lands with clarity and kindness all at once. Try it. You'll find how hard it is. Hard, but always worth the attempt.

Paradigm

Knowing how the slaves and wives, who are specially addressed in the previous section, were to respond in the midst of suffering was formed in the crucible of the physical, verbal, and status abuse, and crucifixion of Jesus Christ at the hand of the Roman authorities in Jerusalem. Peter appealed to that paradigm when advising slaves (2:18–25), and today's passage is very much like what Peter said to the slaves. His opening words in 3:18 "For Christ also suffered" sound like the opening words at 2:21: "because Christ suffered for you."

Peter can't leave the suffering with Christ at the cross of injustice. So, he wanders from the pastoral connection of the suffering of his readers into his favorite theme: the redemptive work of Jesus. So, Jesus suffered for us as a paradigm of suffering becomes, as if an instinct, "once for our sins" (3:18). With that Peter forgets the sufferings of believers and enters into a reflection that many think may have been lines from an early Christian song about salvation in Christ:

> Because Christos suffered, once for all sins.
> The right one for the wrongdoing ones,
> So he might lead you to God,
> Having died in the flesh,
> Being made alive in spirit (3:18; *Second Testament*).

The terseness of expression, more noticeable in the translation above, and the cadence strike many as poetic lines, either drawn from an early Christian song or from Peter's own poetic moment. The first three lines provide the foundation for all atonement theories: Jesus died for "all sins," and he did so vicariously. He is the "right one" and we are the "wrongdoing ones." Fleming Rutledge offers to us the ultimate human warning: "The one great mistake we could make today is to think of ourselves in the wrong category" (Rutledge, "Enemy Lines," 346). Only Jesus is the right one. His purpose was that "he might lead you to God." What we see in 3:18–22 clarifies that the journey to God with Jesus Christ includes the declaration of victory over Satan, sin, and systemic injustices.

At this point, Peter enters into unknown territory, and it can be immediately confusing. I will try to sort out the basics. First, Jesus descended to the place of the dead, called Hades, and "announced" (*Second Testament*) something "to the spirits in prison." A once popular view, that this announcing occurred after the resurrection and in the journey of his ascension to the Father, is less likely. Second, those to whom Jesus announced something are called "imprisoned spirits" and then they are clarified as those who died in the days of Noah (3:19–20). The descent into hell (or Hades) has been a part of the Christian tradition from the early days of the church, and it is taught in today's reading. Joel Green points us to C.S. Lewis's famous scene in *The Lion, the Witch, and the Wardrobe*, in which we read "when a willing victim who had committed no treachery was killed in a traitor's stead, the Table would crack and Death itself would start working backwards" (Green, *1 Peter*, 130). What a wonderful way of speaking of Jesus' entering into Hades to defeat death and offer liberation for the spirits chained. (By the way, C.S. Lewis's first book, written before he was a believer, was called *Spirits in Bondage*.)

Noah built the ark, which saved eight family members through water. Third, this leads Peter into another sidebar, that water is like baptism which now saves persons. But the new baptism is not a physical, but a spiritual, cleansing (3:20–21). That baptism "saves you by the resurrection of Jesus Christ" (3:21). For sure, for many this is unknown territory. Let me clarify that for the earliest Christians, both Jews and gentiles, who all had been nurtured into many rituals involving water, to have become a Christian and not gone through some cleansing ritual would have been impossible. For them, they were saved when they were baptized—not because the water itself saves, but because entrance into the water embodied faith in the cleansing work of Christ.

And fourth, Peter returns to the journey of Christ with "who has gone into heaven" and now occupies a royal seat "at God's right hand" (3:22). What ends today's passage, however, deserves a little scrutiny and connection: "with angels, authorities and powers in submission [same word as 2:13, 18; 3:1] to him" (3:22). Why does Peter bring up these powers? Here's why: Christ's crucifixion, resurrection, and ascension was a *victory over all evil, sin, and systemic structures of oppression.* All have been conquered: sinners in the there and then, the dead of the past, and the powers at work to wreak injustice in this world. Christ's victory is complete. To complicate this just a bit, we add from 4:6, "For this is the reason the gospel was preached," back in 3:19–20, "to those who are now dead." It is a fact that the early church believed when Jesus died that Jesus invaded Hades and wreaked destruction on sin and death and liberated people on the basis of his atoning work. Matthew 27:52–53 illustrate what happened when Jesus entered into the realm of the dead.

At the cross Jesus conquered sin; in the grave he descended into Hades to conquer more sin; in his resurrection and ascension he declared victory over all sin and systemic evil. The work of Christ, once he sat at the right hand, had achieved the Father's mission. We await the final victory.

Peter wandered from his pastoral point about Christ as a paradigm for those suffering, but he will resume his instructions about suffering when we turn to the next passage.

QUESTIONS FOR REFLECTION AND APPLICATION

1. What kinds of sufferings were Peter's recipients likely experiencing?

2. How can kindness be used to re-form systems toward justice, without devolving into tolerating abuse and injustice?

3. What might faithfulness in the midst of suffering look like in balancing the acceptance of normal human emotions while holding on to faith and devotion?

4. How does Jesus' death work to overcome suffering and oppression?

5. Knowing that Jesus has achieved victory over all evil and death, how can you change your perspective on the suffering you face in your life?

FOR FURTHER READING

Alister McGrath, C.S. *Lewis: A Life* (Carol Stream: Tyndale, 2013).

Fleming Rutledge, "The Enemy Lines are Hard to Find," in William H. Willimon, ed., *Sermons from Duke Chapel: Voices from 'A Great Towering Church'* (Durham: Duke University Press, 2005), 342–47.

Leo Tolstoy, "What Men Live By," in *Collected Shorter Fiction*, volume 1 (Everyman's Library 243; New York: A.A. Knopf, 2001), 755–778.

SUFFERING AND NEW LIFE COMMUNITY

1 Peter 4:1–11

¹ Therefore, since Christ suffered in his body, arm yourselves also with the same attitude, because whoever suffers in the body is done with sin. ² As a result, they do not live the rest of their earthly lives for evil human desires, but rather for the will of God. ³ For you have spent enough time in the past doing what pagans choose to do—living in debauchery, lust, drunkenness, orgies, carousing and detestable idolatry. ⁴ They are surprised that you do not join them in their reckless, wild living, and they heap abuse on you. ⁵ But they will have to give account to him who is ready to judge the living and the dead. ⁶ For this is the reason the gospel was preached even to those who are now dead, so that they might be judged according to human standards in regard to the body, but live according to God in regard to the spirit.

⁷ The end of all things is near. Therefore be alert and of sober mind so that you may pray. ⁸ Above all, love each other deeply, because love covers over a multitude of sins. ⁹ Offer hospitality to one another without grumbling. ¹⁰ Each of you should use whatever

gift you have received to serve others, as faithful stewards of God's
grace in its various forms. [11] If anyone speaks, they should do so
as one who speaks the very words of God. If anyone serves, they
should do so with the strength God provides, so that in all things
God may be praised through Jesus Christ. To him be the glory and
the power for ever and ever. Amen.

The section in 1 Peter that began back at 3:13 extends
through 4:19. The instructions set a new way of life for
believers in the context of suffering. Suffering is the con*text*
but not the con*tent*. In 3:13–22, Peter drew their attention
to suffering but he quickly shifted to how to respond and
whom they were to follow (Jesus). In today's reading, suffering appears yet again, but only to say that its deepest damage
is not to the body of the believer but to sin in the life of
believers. With suffering-erasing-sin behind them they are to
be formed into a new life community. Peter splits their life
into two stages: their past life and their present life.

SUFFERING'S IMPACT

Many are surprised by Peter's words in the first verse. The
believers are to arm themselves arm with the same attitude
as Christ had when he suffered (cf. 2:21–23). Even more,
as Christ's death slayed the agent of death (sin), so "the
[believer] who suffered in the flesh has stopped sins" (4:1;
Second Testament). Suffering in the faith unites a believer
with the Suffering Servant, who put sin to death.

Of course, most of us will be asking *Does this mean sinlessness?* Peter answers this question, beginning at verse two,
but before we get there this needs to be said: no Christian in
the New Testament arrived at total sanctification or complete
holiness or absolute love. No one. Jesus had to rebuke the
disciples; the apostles write letters telling good church

people *not to do* one thing after another *because some were no doubt doing such things.* Here's the point: there is a clear distinction, at least when one looks back over time, between a person's past life before Christ and a person's present life with Christ. That's what Peter means by "has stopped sins." Not sinlessness, but abandoning a former life of sin, which he is about to describe in vivid detail.

THEIR PAST

The sin that stopped points at their former reckless life of sin (4:3). The NIV labels them "pagans" but the term is used for "ethnic groups" (*Second Testament*) other than Jews, that is, gentiles. In leaving the gentiles, these believers do not become Jews either. They become a new family with a new life, but they are part of the Abrahamic family formed by a covenant with Israel's God.

Peter provides, much like Paul in Romans 1:18–32 or 1 Corinthians 6:9–10, a profile of the notorious sins of notorious sinners. He puts on the bulletin board some yellow sticky notes in all caps, that is in exaggerated terms, how gentiles live. Not always, but often enough for them to acquire the terms. Two summary expressions are mentioned: first, "human desires" (4:2; *Second Testament*) gets some paraphrastic expansions in the NIV's "evil human desires"; second, "dissolution-flood" (4:4; *Second Testament*) pictures a river overrunning its banks with irredeemable living. The NIV's "reckless, wild living" does the job well. Between these two expressions, Peter details what each of these mean: "flaunting sensualities, desires, wine-soaking, parties, symposia bashes, and non-observant idolatries (4:3; *Second Testament*). That pretty well says all one needs to know. To flaunt is to show off; to flout is to blow through the rules. Either could be attached to their sensualities. The two major patterns of sin of most concern to the apostles for gentile converts were sensualities and idolatries. Both shaped the past of Peter's churches.

One more is added, but it pertains to their present.

THEIR PRESENT

"They heap abuse on you" (4:4 end). The term that needs translation here is *blasphēmeō*, and it can point at language that abuses God (blasphemy) or language that abuses others. I left the term undetermined in *The Second Testament* with "insulting." I believe this term could echo the "detestable idolatry" of 4:3 or it could describe how the believers' former party partners now verbally abuse them. Peter's warning is indirect since he informs the believers of God's judgment on their former, now-unrepentant companions in sensualities and idolatries. Which is why the gospel has been preached to them and to the dead, probably when Christ descended into Hades (see pp. 94–95).

That past is now behind them; they live in a new era, the time of Christ. Peter's opening to verse seven sounds like Jesus (Matthew 10:23; Mark 9:1), like Paul (Romans 13:12), like James (5:9), and like John (Revelation 22:20). Peter's similar wording is: "The end of all things is near" or "has come close" in the sense of closing in on us (1 Peter 4:7). The earliest Christians lived in the expectation of the imminent return of Christ. The prophets of Israel, Judah, and the early church, including Jesus, were not granted a vision of every detail in the future. They were granted what they needed for their day. What they all did was cast their final vision of the kingdom of God right up against the present day, give or a take a generation or two. Peter joins the prophets here. That hope shaped how they lived, and it looked like this:

First, *alertness*. In view of the return of Christ, Peter summons them to "have sensible thoughts and be sober in prayers" (4:7; *Second Testament*). Probably because of their past sensualities in drunkenness, Peter once again urges mental control (cf. 1:13). Mental control here is not about the stoic denial of emotions, but the capacity to regulate one's desires and turn away from one's temptations.

A second trait of living in light of the return of Christ is *devotion to community life*: "having a stretched love for one another" (4:8; *Second Testament*; cf. 1:22) and "offering hospitality to one another" (4:8), a remarkably consistent feature of first century Christianity (cf. Acts 2:46; Romans 14:1–15:13). As can be seen in the Romans passage at 14:1, the hospitality was to be done for Peter's churches "without grumbling" (1 Peter 4:9). Perhaps he has in mind quarreling or perhaps he's thinking of generosity in offering hospitality rather than seeing it as a begrudging duty. Joshua Jipp, a professor of New Testament, poked the ribs of the church when he wanted to get across the importance of hospitality in the New Testament. So, he titled his book *Saved by Faith and Hospitality*! Hospitality embodied the heart of the movement of those following Jesus.

As a community waiting for Christ, they are to *live for one another* in offering their (Spirit-prompted?) gifts of speaking and serving for the good of one another and in light of their callings from God (4:10–12). Just like Paul: whatever "gift" they have been given by God's grace, they are to use "to serve others" (4:10).

Such a life in light of the return of Christ, all is to be done *to glorify or splendor God*. We use the term "doxology" for these acts of praise. The gifts we exercise come from God and are done in the "strength God provides," so they are to be done in praise to God, who is worthy of our doxological life: "to him be the glory [*doxa*] and the power for ever and ever." And Peter prompts the believers to say "Amen" (4:11).

Questions for Reflection
and Application

1. What is the difference between full sinlessness and stopping a life of sin?

2. How does Peter's list of stereotypical sins serve to illustrate the differences in life before and after Jesus for the believers?

3. How does Peter want the believers to discipline their thoughts and lifestyle choices?

4. What role should hospitality play in the life of these believers?

5. Think about your life before and after Jesus. What characterized it before? What characterizes it now?

FOR FURTHER READING

Joshua J. Jipp, *Saved by Faith and Hospitality* (Grand Rapids: Wm. B. Eerdmans, 2017). For my brief summary: https://www.patheos .com/blogs/jesuscreed/2017/08/23/salvation -hospitality-alone/

SUFFERING AND GOD

1 Peter 4:12–19

[12] *Dear friends, do not be surprised at the fiery ordeal that has come on you to test you, as though something strange were happening to you.* [13] *But rejoice inasmuch as you participate in the sufferings of Christ, so that you may be overjoyed when his glory is revealed.* [14] *If you are insulted because of the name of Christ, you are blessed, for the Spirit of glory and of God rests on you.* [15] *If you suffer, it should not be as a murderer or thief or any other kind of criminal, or even as a meddler.* [16] *However, if you suffer as a Christian, do not be ashamed, but praise God that you bear that name.* [17] *For it is time for judgment to begin with God's household; and if it begins with us, what will the outcome be for those who do not obey the gospel of God?*

[18] *And,*

> *"If it is hard for the righteous to be saved,*
> *what will become of the ungodly and the sinner?"*

[19] *So then, those who suffer according to God's will should commit themselves to their faithful Creator and continue to do good.*

Peter has wandered three times away from his discussion of believers suffering only to discuss Christ's redemption and the Christian life in the midst of suffering. His wanderings prevented him from completing what he had begun saying about suffering. So, his next set of instructions allows him to finish his instructions about suffering. This time, Peter frames suffering in the providence of God.

Before we turn to the passage, a brief observation. I believe God is sovereign, but I also believe God, for God's own reasons, has given considerable freedom to humans. Furthermore, in some sense God set the universe to spinning and expanding and adjusting according to the logic of divine providence. But all this is part of God's design and the human experience. At the heart of the human experience is making sense of God's world, and at the heart of divine revelation is the story of Israel. Peter wants the Christians to understand their experience in the context of how God works in the world. God's work finds its defining story in the story of Israel and Israel's scriptures. In our passage, Peter alludes to Isaiah 11:2 in verse fourteen, and he quotes Proverbs 11:31 in verse eighteen. These texts set up the experience of suffering in the grand story of God's people.

Some people have the need, tendency, and edginess of a theology that wants to explain everything that happens by what they believe God is doing to them or for them, and they offer at times precise ideas of why God is doing what God is doing. They believe God causes, at some level, everything that happens. This view is sometimes named "meticulous sovereignty." Here's an example: a job offer requires a parent or both parents to move to another state, to different schools for their children, to cause a disruption of friendships and fellowship. Attribution theory explains it like this: God wants us to move to this state, God wants our children to change schools, and God has willed for us to leave our friends and form new ones. This is God's specific plan for us. All this disruption can lead this family to grow in their trust of God, but it can also be deeply damaging for a long time to one or more family members. This situation is on the scale of weightiness rather innocent, and I'm not diminishing the pain for some in the family. When we turn to something weightier, what happens to one's view of God and God's sovereignty when a six-year-old dies of cancer? Or when a teenager is sexually assaulted? Or when a young girl is kidnapped and trafficked? Attribution theory, which is the tendency to attribute everything in life to God's immutably willed plan, in these cases is forced to attribute evil and injustices to God. But this view of God won't work for the God revealed in Jesus Christ. It is far wiser and does not lead to profound theological error in attributing evil to God, to say instead that a family has learned to trust in God from the experience. It is even wiser to say God never plotted and caused evil actions and horrific experiences to happen, but it is our calling to live faithfully and compassionately, with lament and grief and complaint, through our sufferings.

All to say, the various sufferings of the Christians in Asia Minor were not God dishing out verbal abuses and physical attacks. Rather than blaming God, Peter *explains how the believers can learn from what is happening so they can grow in faithfulness.*

SUFFERING, ONE MORE TIME

Three expressions are used to describe their suffering. The obvious, "suffer" (4:16), and a specific instance of suffering, "insulted" (4:14), and then a wide-ranging framing of the whole experience: "the fiery ordeal that has come on you to test you" (4:12). The only specific here is verbal insults.

Such insults were shaped to degrade a person, to gaslight a person, to humiliate, to sealion, and to cause the person to disappear.

We can draw together the suffering *because they are Christians* in this letter. Notice these:

"as you participate in the sufferings of Christ" (4:13).

"because of the name of Christ" (4:14).

"if you suffer as a Christian" (4:16).

"that you bear that name" (4:16).

Much of their suffering seems to have been verbal. However, "fiery trial" seems more severe than verbal insults and the beating of the slaves, but their faith factored into why it was happening. Again, as Joel Green exquisitely says it, "this suffering in the service of God's will ought not to be read as a claim by the apostle that God wills suffering, but rather that serving the will of God in a disbelieving world has suffering as its potential (sometimes probable) outcome" (Green, *1 Peter*, 159). Green makes the right connections: doing God's will and suffering for doing God's will.

FRAMING SUFFERING

Since Peter knows suffering, he knows what it does to the person: it can be framed as a "test" (4:12). Peter also could not avoid remembering when he failed the test of his faith in the courtyard when Jesus was put on trial (Mark 14:66–72). Faith failure followed by repentance and resumption of the walk of faith are not unusual for believers. The letter of James explains what Peter means by test:

Consider it pure joy, my brothers and sisters, whenever you face trials of many kinds, because you know
that the testing of your faith produces perseverance.
Let perseverance finish its work so that you may be
mature and complete, not lacking anything. If any
of you lacks wisdom, you should ask God, who gives
generously to all without finding fault, and it will be
given to you. (James 1:2–5)

One needs wisdom from God to discern how to respond
to suffering, but suffering has a way of testing that leads to
strengthening faith. Bad experiences in life—cancer, death in
a family, divorce, failing at a vocational application one wanted
deeply—when they are turned over to God in prayer, in coun-
sel with the wise, and with the patient learning in humility,
have proven over and over to be tests that taught us much.

The content of this test is explained before the test is
given: they can take joy before the test because they know
they get to "participate in the sufferings of Christ" (4:13).
The famous words of Dietrich Bonhoeffer explain what Peter
means: "Those who enter into discipleship enter into Jesus'
death. They turn their living into dying; such has been the
case from the very beginning. The cross is not the terrible
end of a pious, happy life. Instead, it stands at the beginning
of community with Jesus Christ. Whenever Christ calls us,
his call leads us to death." Two pages later he wrote, "But how
should disciples know what their cross is? They will receive
it when they begin to follow the suffering Lord. They will
recognize their cross in communion with Jesus" (Bonhoeffer,
Discipleship, 87, 89). Peter intensifies the connection to
Christ by saying they are now "blessed" because they are
united with Christ in their suffering (4:14). The Spirit is all
over them—"Rests on you"—to comfort (as Paraclete; John
14:16, 26; 15:26; 16:7) and to empower them.

That frame of testing will lead, Peter confidently affirms, to their being full of blubbering with joy. His words are "so that you may rejoice, overjoying, at his splendorous apocalypse" (4:13; *Second Testament*). Framing suffering by hope does not suffocate one's feelings nor does it pretend things are all peachy-keen or just or even acceptable. Rather, knowing that God will make all things right can relieve some of the pain while giving us a fresh angle on what we experience.

Peter goes all-out grim at the end of today's reading: "for it is time for judgment to begin," and here Peter pulls us back to 4:7's "the end of all things is near." Like the other apostles, Peter believed the kingdom could be at hand. But that's not grim like his next words: "and it begins with us" (4:17). I hear this expression often today because of the church's systemic dysfunctions paraded in newspapers, magazine, and websites: "We are in a day of reckoning." (Note 1 Corinthians 11:32.) Yes, I suppose we are. Peter surely thought the sufferings of the church could be framed as God beginning a universal judgment on all creation. The piercing judgment of God will make clear who is faithful and who is not. Peter's grimness goes darker with an indirect warning: "if it begins with us, what will the outcome be for those who do not obey the gospel of God?" (4:17). Those words remind Peter of Proverbs 11:31, which he quotes in 4:18. In other words, he must have wondered if Revelation 6–16 was just over the horizon!

WHAT TO DO?

First, Christians in the first century needed to be reminded that they should not think the fiery ordeal of suffering "is a foreign thing" to the ways of Christ (*Second Testament*, 4:12). And in our passage Peter at times sounds like Jesus in Matthew 5:10–12. Surely, they knew this, and at least they knew from what has been said in the letter, starting with the sixth and seventh verses of the first chapter. Second, they could actually see through the awfulnesses of their experiences into the future world of justice and rejoice (4:13). Third, he writes "do not be ashamed." Instead, they are "to praise God that you bear that name," namely the name of Jesus Christ (4:16). By the way, 4:16 is one of three passages in the New Testament where followers of Jesus are called "Christians" (see Acts 11:26; 26:28). Fourth, the last verse of today's passage can be translated to form into one instead of two practices: "So then, those who suffer according to God's will should *commit themselves to their faithful Creator and continue to do good*" (4:19). Surrendering oneself to God while doing what is good is Peter's overall strategy. One more time Peter tells them to continue to do "good deeds." This draws us back all over to the strategy of 2:12: "Live such good lives among the pagans that, though they accuse you [falsely] of doing wrong, they may see your good deeds and glorify God on the day he visits us."

QUESTIONS FOR REFLECTION AND APPLICATION

1. How does the story of God's people in Israel inform Peter's understanding and explanation of suffering?

2. Compare the wording in Matthew 5:10–12 to 1 Peter 4:13–14. What terms seem to be the same or similar?

3. What is the difference between "God causes suffering" and "doing God's will" might have suffering as an outcome?

4. How might Peter's failure to remain faithful in the face of verbal attacks at Jesus' trial impact his words to the believers in his letter?

5. How does attribution theory explain the things that happen in life in relation to God's will? Do you or have you believed this approach? How did that belief impact you?

FOR FURTHER READING

Dietrich Bonhoeffer, *Discipleship* (Dietrich Bonhoeffer Works 4; Minneapolis: Fortress, 2001).

MENTORS FOR YOUNGER LEADERS

1 Peter 5:1–14

¹ To the elders among you, I appeal as a fellow elder and a witness of Christ's sufferings who also will share in the glory to be revealed: ² Be shepherds of God's flock that is under your care, watching over them—not because you must, but because you are willing, as God wants you to be; not pursuing dishonest gain, but eager to serve; ³ not lording it over those entrusted to you, but being examples to the flock. ⁴ And when the Chief Shepherd appears, you will receive the crown of glory that will never fade away.

⁵ In the same way, you who are younger, submit yourselves to your elders. All of you, clothe yourselves with humility toward one another, because,

> "God opposes the proud
> but shows favor to the humble."

⁶ Humble yourselves, therefore, under God's mighty hand, that he may lift you up in due time. ⁷ Cast all your anxiety on him because he cares for you.

⁸ Be alert and of sober mind. Your enemy the devil prowls around like a roaring lion looking for someone to devour. ⁹ Resist

him, standing firm in the faith, because you know that the family of believers throughout the world is undergoing the same kind of sufferings.

[10] And the God of all grace, who called you to his eternal glory in Christ, after you have suffered a little while, will himself restore you and make you strong, firm and steadfast. [11] To him be the power for ever and ever. Amen.

[12] With the help of Silas, whom I regard as a faithful brother, I have written to you briefly, encouraging you and testifying that this is the true grace of God. Stand fast in it.

[13] She who is in Babylon, chosen together with you, sends you her greetings, and so does my son Mark. [14] Greet one another with a kiss of love.

Peace to all of you who are in Christ.

For those who pay attention to such things, it may shock some not to hear about the leaders of these churches across Asia Minor until the "last page" of this letter. So much attention in our churches today is directed at pastors, at senior pastors, and at preachers and teachers that some might have expected a word for the leaders to begin the letter. To this day, communications with churches tend to be top-down, starting with pastors and priests before the congregation hears anything. Peter addresses all the people first, and only at the end turns to the "elders." Perhaps this letter illustrates a bottom-up perception of the church. I'm not sure we can infer such from the organization of this letter, but thinking about such is a good place to begin our last reflection on 1 Peter.

Dennis Edwards pastored for decades before becoming a seminary professor and administrator. His opening words on this passage are golden, and I want to quote a longer section and hope that you, especially if you are involved in leadership at a church, read them slowly:

Most of my education, for which I am grateful, focused on handling Scripture, understanding theological ideas, appreciating the history of Christianity, and also communicating through preaching and teaching. But churches apparently do not expect their pastors to be resident theologians, counselors, or even teachers. Modern-day pastors are expected to be motivational speakers with managerial skills akin to those of American business professionals. I have attended gatherings on leadership in the church which featured plenty of presentations from the business and political worlds, while studies from Scripture were absent or minimal. Additionally, the current tendency is to laud as successful those who manage with what approaches a dictatorship. (Edwards, *1 Peter*, 199)

Exactly. Those words are from a (former) pastor who knows. I put former in parentheses because you can take a pastor from the church to be a professor, but you can't take the pastor out of the professor. Dennis is a wise, humble leader whose approach to teaching and pastoring counter the approaches of too many today (Edwards, *Humility Illuminated*).

VIRTUES FOR AN ELDER

The job description for a pastor today has morphed from a spiritual director and Bible teacher/theologian to an organizational leader, manager, and entrepreneur. I have spent hours reading such descriptions in an effort to come to terms not only with the church today but also with what students expect of themselves on the basis of this morphed pastoral calling. When a pastor sees himself (this is mostly a male game when it comes to the newer sense of a pastor) as a leader, a manager, or an entrepreneur, those visions, mostly culled and adjusted from the business world, will shape what the pastor does and what the church becomes.

Leadership, managing, and even vision-casting form part of the pastoral calling. What concerns me, and I stand here on the shoulders of Eugene Peterson, who in book after book griped about the morphing of the pastoral image from a spiritual director to an administrative leader, is that in the process the paradigmatic images of the pastor in the Bible get lost (see Peterson, *Pastor*). It all begins right here, or it goes astray quickly: the people are not the pastor's, and the pastor should not speak of "my" church; the people are "God's flock" (1 Peter 5:2). If it is God's flock, then God is the Shepherd. To pastor/shepherd, then, is to participate in the work of God, in the work of the Good Shepherd named Jesus, and here are some passages to explore: Psalm 23, Jeremiah 23:1–4, Ezekiel 34, Zechariah 11, Matthew 9:35–38, and John 10. It's ery much worth your pausing to read again as Jesus appoints Peter to become a pastor in John 21. Peter, in today's passage, uses formative terms—fellow elder, witness, shepherd—because they, under Jesus, co-pastor and co-mentor God's people (see Titus 1:5–9). He indicates then the marks of a mentor, and here I quote from my translation of 1 Peter 5:2–3:

> *Pastor* God's flock among you, *mentoring,*
> *not from necessity* but *willingly,*
> *consistent with God,*
> *not for shameful gain* but *emotionally,*
> *not as ruling over* the part [assigned to you]
> but becoming *models* for the flock.
> (McKnight, *Second Testament*)

I have italicized the sorts of words used that formed persons into the pastoral calling. What they were not to be were people who did their job because they had to, who performed their jobs to get paid or to get wealthy, or who saw themselves as controllers or dominant. Instead, they were to pastor—which means to care for people in providing, in protecting, and in guiding—and to mentor, the typical term often translated with "overseer" or "watching over" (NIV). They were to mentor people in the Christian faith because they wanted to, which points to a renewed will by the power of the Spirit. They were to mentor in a manner "consistent with God" (NIV: "as God wants"), and this draws us to the routine use of God as a shepherd in the Old Testament (see Ezekiel 34 especially). They were to mentor people "emotionally," which the NIV translates "eager to serve." The Greek term is *prothumōs*, and if one breaks it apart it means heated passion for something or someone and can even suggest "freely" (Green, *1 Peter*, 166).

Leadership roles like pastoring, mentoring, elder-ing, and deacon-ing, not to ignore preaching, have a habit of attracting people who like the stage, the platform, the performance, the glory, and the power. This has been the case in the church since Simon the sorcerer in Act 8:9–25, who was knocked off the platform by none other than Peter. Perhaps he's why Peter wrote in 1 Peter 5:3 (*Second Testament*), "not ruling over the part assigned to you," with the "part" referring to the small church the person was called to mentor. Peter's term is strong: "not ruling," lording it over, or domineering or dominating. Christian mentoring is not about power over others but about sharing power with others and empowering others. Finally, the essence of Christian virtue is being the kind of person who becomes a "model" or an example for others to follow. But only insofar as a mentor follows the example of Christ (2:21). That's what struck Barbara Brown Taylor about her pastor, and it led her to become a pastor. She wrote about her childhood pastor in these terms: "He seemed able, when he looked at me, to see a person and not only a child, and I loved him for it" (*The Preaching Life*, 15).

Mentoring others in the way of Christ requires patience, love, and, well, more than the ordinary amount of patience. In P.D. James's wonderful novel, *Death in Holy Orders*, we read about pastoral visitation in the most realistic of terms:

> He had returned from two hours of visiting long-term sick and housebound parishioners. As always he had tried conscientiously to meet their individual and predictable needs: blind Mrs. Oliver, who liked him to read a passage of scripture and pray with her; old Sam Possinger, who on every visit re-fought the Battle of Alamein; Mrs. Poley, caged in her Zimmer frame, avid for the latest parish gossip; Carl Lomas, who had never set foot in St. Botolph's but liked discussing theology and the defects of the Church of England. Mrs. Poley, with his help, had edged her way painfully into the kitchen and made tea, taking from the tin the gingerbread cake she had baked for him. He had unwisely praised it four years ago, on his first visit, and was now condemned to eat it weekly, finding it impossible to admit that he disliked gingerbread. But the tea, hot and strong, had been welcome and would save him the trouble of making it at home. (James, *Death in Holy Orders*, 166)

What is absent in Peter's brief section for mentors is perhaps the #1 skill many churches measure: preaching. Not one word about it here. The only truly verbal skill mentioned is being a "witness" (5:1), which is, first of all, about Peter's own life but indirectly about his fellow mentors throughout Asia Minor. Peter observed the "sufferings of Christ" and lived to tell others what he saw. A witness is a see-then-say or an

125

experience-then-say term. If this term extends to the mentors, then they are to be witnesses of their own experience with Christ. Included in Peter's witness about Christ were lessons he saw and heard from Jesus (Mark 9:33–37; 10:35–45). Being a witness reshapes the preaching task from standing *in the place of God* before the congregation to standing *to the side* while pointing people to Jesus himself. The preacher constantly is tempted to shift from being a witness to being the voice of God. The true witness to Christ enables people to hear the voice of God because the witness's voice is swallowed by the voice of Christ. Frederick Buechner, pastor and novelist, once wrote about preaching, evoking (without saying it) the vital importance of personal witness in these terms:

> If preachers or lecturers are to say anything that really matters to anyone including themselves, they must say it not just to the public part of us that considers interesting thoughts about the Gospel and how to preach it, but to the private, inner part too, to the part of us all where our dreams come from, both our good dreams and our bad dreams, the inner part where thoughts mean less than images, elucidation less than evocation, where our concern is less with how the Gospel is to be preached than with what the Gospel is and what it is to us. (Buechner, *Telling the Truth*, 4)

To be a witness is to reveal one's inner world. But it can go too far and that is why we need these wise words from a well-known pastor who became a professor of pastors, Will Willimon:

> It is not my task primarily to "share myself" with my people, certainly not to heed the facile advice of those who say, "Just be yourself." (As Mark Twain said,

that's about the worst advice one can give anybody.)
Fortunately, as I enter into the struggles of my people,
I have considerably more to offer than myself. I have
the witness of the saints, the faith of the church, the
wisdom of the ages. (Willimon, *Pastor*, 21)

Another temptation for the preacher is to tell too many
stories about themselves. A witness points to Jesus; a story-
teller to himself or herself.

What may surprise even more is the *absence of women*
in 1 Peter 5's instructions to mentors and wannabe mentors.
One can think of several possible explanations. Perhaps there
were no women leaders, but this would be next to impossible.
Maybe Peter saw instructions of women in the mentors and
younger persons, which is a generous and possible reading.
Possibly women were invisible to him. I have a hard time
accepting that women were invisible to Peter. I would like to
think Peter had women in mind in the "younger" of 5:5, but
the term is masculine and more in line with younger men.
Yet the term could be inclusive and mean younger men and
women. The NIV's "younger" leaves it open.

Another absence worth mentioning here is the vulnera-
bility of the pastor and the pastor's family to the gossip and
wounding words of parishioners. Willa Cather, my favorite
American novelist in my favorite novel of hers, put the dangers of gossip into words with these: "The fear of the tongue,
that terror of little towns, is usually felt more keenly by the
minister's family than by other households" (*The Song of the
Lark*, 116).

VIRTUES FOR YOUNGER FOLKS

A door is cracked enough for us to peek in to see that some
young persons were in the process of being mentored by

mentors, perhaps so they could mentor someday. But as above, perhaps Peter only has younger persons (men and women) in view, and future leadership is not the issue. All Peter tells these "younger" folks is to adjust their way of living to the older mentors. Age matters because it grants experience, maturation, and wisdom. This is not ageism, either for the elderly or against the younger generation, but age-as-wisdom.

Let's take the verse referring to potential leaders for the sake of the following: Every young person who wants to become a pastor-mentor needs at least two or three mentors who have decades of experience with a solid, caring, wise reputation. To "submit" here does not mean *do whatever they say*, and those who imply that's what submit means are the ones a young person needs to avoid as a mentor. Find a few mentors and bask in their wisdom.

VIRTUES FOR ALL

Paragraph divisions were not part of the original letter. The NIV's decision to connect "All of you" seamlessly with his address to the "younger" clouds a reading. The virtues of all carries on from 5:5b through verse nine.

Lists of things to do, or rules for life, or even commands and prohibitions, more often than not, are *symptoms of virtue* more than cataloging what one needs to do. In other words, the what-to-dos are more about what-to-bes. A mature, wise, and virtuous Christian, then, is often observed being humble (5:5b–6). As Dennis Edwards defines it, "Humility is a way of life rooted in submission to God and is demonstrated in actions that foster mutuality rather than competition" (Edwards, *Humility Illuminated*, 3). What comes into play can be missed in the Western world. Honor and shame, status and degradation of one's honor, fired as they each are by competitions and contests, are all antagonizing one another here. Those on the margin of society, as at least some of the readers of this original letter were, as well as those who had a decent status in society were experiencing status degradation for following Jesus. Their lowering of status will be flipped because God will "lift" them up "in due time" (5:6).

Handling one's emotional difficulties is both a process and a sign of Christian virtue. Thus, Peter speaks of tossing one's *disturbances* on God, a term often translated with "anxieties." To pose anxiety as a moral defect unfortunately wounds those who have diagnoses of anxiety. The idea is one's inner world becoming disturbed or turbulent or agitated. The agitated, Peter said at 1:13, need to be "alert and of sober mind" (5:8), but here he adds what lurks: "Your adversary, the Accuser" haunts you (and us). The antidote to the Accuser's lurking to swallow us up is to resist by firming up one's faith, by becoming alert to the Accuser's presence, by recognizing its furtive temptations, and by turning from that presence and those temptations. What empowers the resister is knowing that the family of faith all over the world is on our side. The internet provides us a form of Christian support 24/7 all over the world, while at the same time the Accuser's presence pervades the internet.

The God who sends the Chief Shepherd back to be with us and so reward faithfulness (5:4), the God who "opposes the proud" and has a preferential option for the humble (5:5), the God who has a "mighty hand" (5:6), the God who raises the status of the humble (5:6), the God who cares for us (5:7), is the "God of all grace" who "will prepare, support, strengthen, and found" us, the latter meaning making us a sure foundation (5:10). The tests of life in this world (1:6–7), which involve suffering for some believers, are to be faced knowing God loves us, is with us, and empowers us. This last term, noticeably, is why Peter closes that little doxology with "To him be the *power* for ever and ever."

BEFORE FOLDING UP A LETTER

Before you and I fold this letter up, hear the final words of Peter. He recognizes those who helped him write this letter, namely, Silas and perhaps Mark (author of the Gospel; 1 Peter 5:12, 13). Peter could have written the letter himself, or he could have had someone write it for him, adding editorial flourishes of his own, or he could have dictated the letter to Silas, or he could have asked Silas to write up a letter expressing what he and Silas and Mark had talked about. We don't know, but something along these lines describes how it worked. What matters is that Peter gives credit where credit is due, and perhaps more than was due.

When Peter mentions "Babylon" he reveals an early Christian perception of the political, religious, moral, and cultural corruptions in Rome, and this was precisely the term exploited by John in Revelation 17–19. He wants them all to greet one with the family greeting of side cheek kisses (1 Peter 5:14). We don't do this in the Midwest, so don't try it on me! Hugs and handshakes get the job done.

Peace.

QUESTIONS FOR REFLECTION
AND APPLICATION

1. What job responsibilities come to mind when you think of a "pastor"?

MENTORS FOR YOUNGER LEADERS

2. How does Christlike shepherding differ from authoritarian leadership for a pastor?

3. Can you think of an example of preacher you've heard who positioned themselves as standing *in the place of God*? Can you think of a preacher you've seen who *stands to the side* and points people to Jesus?

4. Have you ever had a pastor mentor you? What was that experience like for you, whether positive or negative?

5. What does it shift for you to understand Peter saying, "cast your disturbances on him" rather than "cast your anxieties"?

131

FOR FURTHER READING

Frederick Buechner, *Telling the Truth: The Gospel as Tragedy, Comedy, and Fairy Tale* (San Francisco: Harper & Row, 1977).

Willa Cather, *The Song of the Lark* (New York: Random House/Vintage, 1999).

Dennis R. Edwards, *Humility Illuminated: The Biblical Path Back to Christian Character* (Downers Grove: IVP Academic, 2023).

P.D. James, *Death in Holy Orders* (New York: A.A. Knopf, 2001).

Eugene Peterson, *The Pastor: A Memoir* (New York: HarperOne, 2011).

Barbara Brown Taylor, *The Preaching Life* (Lanham, Md.: Cowley, 1993).

Will Willimon, *Pastor: The Theology and Practice of Ordained Ministry* (rev. ed.; Nashville: Abingdon, 2016).

2 PETER

REDEMPTIVE KNOWLEDGE

2 Peter 1:1–2

¹ Simon Peter, a servant and apostle of Jesus Christ,

To those who through the righteousness of our God and Savior Jesus Christ have received a faith as precious as ours:

² Grace and peace be yours in abundance through the knowledge of God and of Jesus our Lord.

Peter, pastors, and parents long for those they love to be transformed into a Christlike life. We all do. We want it for ourselves. This letter taps the keys of transformation from beginning to end. The origin of Christian transformation is the work of God in Jesus Christ, so Peter's opening to his letter, like most letters in the early church, frames redemption as a transforming power available to each of us. Like those other letters, too, Peter scratches onto the papyrus words with considerable weight.

REDEMPTIVE KNOWLEDGE

Salvation is knowledge, the kind of knowledge that leads to transformation in Christian virtues. Peter's fresh developments in his understanding of salvation emphasizes (1) Jesus as Savior (1:1, 11; 2:20; 3:2, 18) and (2) the transformative power of knowledge. What he says in this letter supplements what is taught in 1 Peter.

It begins with where we are and who (or whose) we are. Peter is a slave and an apostle of Jesus Christ (1:1). The word slave ironically exalts Peter in the Jewish and Christian traditions (cf. Deuteronomy 34:5; 2 Samuel 3:18). He envisions his audience in theological categories: "To those who through the righteousness of our God and Savior Jesus Christ have received a faith as precious as ours" (1:1). These terms for his audience are piled on top of one another, and I have translated them as follows: "To the ones designated with an equally-honorable-for [or with]-us allegiance in the rightness of our God and Deliverer, Yēsous Christos" (*Second Testament*). The term "allegiance" corresponds to the NIV's "faith," which is the beginning of redemptive knowledge, not unlike Proverb's sketch of wisdom originating in the fear of God. That Peter connects "God" with "Savior" as he does, and Savior to "Jesus Christ," indicates Peter believes Jesus is God (see John 1:1; Romans 9:5; Titus 2:13; Hebrews 1:8–9).

Peter's audience has an "equally honorable allegiance" to Jesus, which the NIV translates a "faith as precious as ours" (1:1). Precious helps but as a translation more needs to be evident. The Greek word is *isotimos*, coming from "equal" (*iso*) and "honor" (*timos*). Their faith and Peter's faith, and the faith of each who was to receive this letter, are equally honorable. The NIV's "as precious as" is not as precise or social as Peter's language. This is about equality in faith, and this equal faith gives such persons honor before God and with one another. Thus, their social status in the family of Jesus has nothing to do with what the world thinks of them. They are honored by God because they are connected to Jesus Christ.

Such a faith-connection with Jesus forms us into righteousness, a righteousness that comes to us in and through Jesus Christ. Righteousness describes someone or something that corresponds consistently with the character and will of God. We speak of it both as (1) a practice (we grow in righteousness as we follow Jesus), as (2) a character trait or attribute of God and the Lord Jesus (Jesus is the Righteous One), and (3) as a status (in Christ we are righteous because he is righteous). Righteousness then is fundamentally relational: we acquire it only in relation to Christ.

Peter prays they will flourish in both "grace and peace" (1:2). Grace in the New Testament comes to us by an act of the God who loves us, and grace draws us into a relationship of mutual exchange. Our exchange is gratitude, thanksgiving, love, and obedience. Peace points at the inner tranquility that can lead to mutual good relations among one another in the fellowship.

Noticeably their flourishing in both grace and peace occurs "through the knowledge of God and of Jesus our Lord." Perception of the truth about God as the agent of flourishing is quite the claim. I have to say that, as a theologian myself, an emphasis on the power of knowing God and Christ plucks strings of resonance. Too many today pooh-pooh theology and knowledge and study and intellectual distinctions. Yes, we are to give practice a noticeable priority. After all, we experience some who know but don't do, who think but don't love. But those sorts do not replace the importance of knowledge. Instead, we are to prioritize a discipleship that is gospel-informed in such a way that the knowledge yields its God-shaped goal: transformation of character. Redemptive knowledge is so important that I want to record primary instances in this letter of the term "knowledge" to set the tone for what is to come in the rest of this letter:*

Grace and peace be yours in abundance through the *knowledge* of God and of Jesus our Lord (1:2).

His divine power has given us everything we need for a godly life through our *knowledge* of him who called us by his own glory and goodness (1:3).

For this very reason, make every effort to add to your faith goodness; and to goodness, *knowledge*;* and to *knowledge*,* self-control . . . (1:5, 6).

For if you possess these qualities in increasing measure, they will keep you from being ineffective and unproductive in your *knowledge* of our Lord Jesus Christ (1:8).

For we did not follow cleverly devised stories when *we told you*+ about the coming of our Lord Jesus Christ in power, but we were eyewitnesses of his majesty (1:16).

Above all, *you must understand#* that no prophecy of Scripture came about by the prophet's own interpretation of things (1:20).

If they have escaped the corruption of the world by *knowing* our Lord and Savior Jesus Christ and are

---

* Greek terms for knowledge in 2 Peter: *Gnōsis*; +*Gnōrizō*; #*Ginōskō*; *Epiginōskō* unmarked

again entangled in it and are overcome, they are worse off at the end than they were at the beginning (2:20).

Above all, *you must understand*# that in the last days scoffers will come, scoffing and following their own evil desires (3:3).

But grow in the grace and *knowledge** of our Lord and Savior Jesus Christ. To him be glory both now and forever! Amen (3:18).

This letter will work out line after line what redemptive knowledge looks like. As a taste of what it is to come, redemptive knowledge is about Jesus Christ, it is about transformation in virtue, and it is about perceiving false teachings. Each of these become vital themes in 2 Peter, but the larger theme is knowledge of God. Sister Athanasius, a leading character in Lil Copan's precious novel, *Little Hours*, opens a window to let in the sun's light on how knowledge and life work best, writing to her friend Miriam, "Knowing God in each moment simply raises that moment" (Copan, *Little Hours*, 34).

QUESTIONS FOR REFLECTION
AND APPLICATION

1. What does "righteousness" mean to Peter?

2. How does Peter flesh out ideas of understanding and knowledge in this letter?

3. How can knowledge help accomplish transformation of character?

4. What can knowledge do to help believers perceive false teachings?

5. What has helped you gain useful and transformative knowledge in your Christian life?

FOR FURTHER READING

Lil Copan, *Little Hours: A Novel* (Falmouth, Massachusetts: One Bird Books, 2021).

FIT FOR CHRISTIAN DESTINY

2 Peter 1:3–11

³ His divine power has given us everything we need for a godly life through our knowledge of him who called us by his own glory and goodness. ⁴ Through these he has given us his very great and precious promises, so that through them you may participate in the divine nature, having escaped the corruption in the world caused by evil desires.

⁵ For this very reason, make every effort to add to your faith goodness; and to goodness, knowledge; ⁶ and to knowledge, self-control; and to self-control, perseverance; and to perseverance, godliness; ⁷ and to godliness, mutual affection; and to mutual affection, love. ⁸ For if you possess these qualities in increasing measure, they will keep you from being ineffective and unproductive in your knowledge of our Lord Jesus Christ. ⁹ But whoever does not have them is nearsighted and blind, forgetting that they have been cleansed from their past sins.

¹⁰ Therefore, my brothers and sisters, make every effort to confirm your calling and election. For if you do these things, you will never stumble, ¹¹ and you will receive a rich welcome into the eternal kingdom of our Lord and Savior Jesus Christ.

Parents and pastors alike pursue paths to spiritual formation, both for themselves and for those in their care. Words that have the power to attract attention to the secret sauce often begin with words like *Three Keys* or *Five Habits* or *The One Secret*. Not finding the failproof secret has not prevented pursuing one. One of my favorites I first read in high school, a book by the famous UCLA basketball coach, John Wooden: *They Call Me Coach*. In it, he detailed twenty-five personal traits of those who would be successful. He called it the Pyramid of Success, and it can be found at the website https://www.thewoodeneffect.com/pyramid-of-success/. There is a mountain of wisdom in Wooden's Pyramid, and many leaders have used it or adapted it.

Peter's got a similar kind of listing but I fear that today's passage can be read, like so many of such attempts to find a ladder to achieving one's goals, as the secret to transformation. Once some scheme or list is understood as the secret, the teacher promises transformation. Those who fail are too often told they either don't have enough faith, or they are not trying hard enough. It is true that Peter provides a chain of formation in today's reading, but we suggest that this is no new insider secret path but instead an old and wise path.

We have learned from the Industrial Revolution, and Henry Ford, about assembly lines and the order of manufacturing. A similar assembly line theory orders a classic Bible education: first the basic courses in Bible—Old and New Testaments; then Greek and Hebrew, which require beginning Greek and Hebrew and then the more advanced levels of understanding the intricacies of the languages. Having mastered the languages, one can move on to write sophisticated commentary on a text (ideally). Virtue is not so mechanical, even if one can sort out virtues in a hierarchy. Love is more important than showing up on time for work.

But virtue can never be Christian without Christian graces at work in a person. Today's passage gets a special slant if we begin at the end.

CHRISTIAN DESTINY

What's the goal? Such a good question, and the answer to it has been cut in half. The current generation grew up on a gospel that promised heaven, threatened hell, and ironically weakened discipleship for those headed for heaven by promising them heaven regardless of how a person lived. The response to this common past for so many of us has been a stronger commitment to the earth, to justice, and to community. And heaven, or the future kingdom of God, has been depreciated. This newer emphasis on making the most of our life now, if truth be told, flows more consistently from a life of privilege than the kind of life Peter's audiences experienced—frankly, the kind of life many in our world today know.

The final, ultimate destiny, one that as we will see very shortly, reshapes life in the here and now, is "the eternal kingdom," or what I translate as "the Era Empire," that is the Empire that pertains to the Age to Come, the endless era in the future. The Greek word *aiōnion*, often translated "eternal," more accurately means an epoch, an era. Since that era is the final era, and since it is eternal, it is often translated "eternal" (NIV). But that deletes the basal meaning of epoch or era. So, I have tried to inch us back to a better understanding by using Era. The Roman empire, and all human empires, will give way to the final Empire, which is the one over which "our Lord and Savior Jesus Christ" will rule (1:11).

Christian destiny reshapes life now, not by escaping this world, not by devaluing our work or creation, not by demonizing those who are unlike us, but . . . this destiny, *because it is the Empire of Jesus*, is fit only for those who are allegiant to Jesus. Which means those who live in the here and now as followers of Jesus, which is precisely what Peter writes about in today's passage. The kingdom is outfitted for those who have been transformed over time, for those whose life looks something like what Peter maps in verses five through eight.

CHRISTIAN GRACES

Those fit for a Christian destiny have experienced the grace of "divine power" through the grace of a redemptive "knowledge" of the God who "called us by his own glory and goodness" (1:3). They know that destiny as another grace, God's "honorable and great pledges" (1:4, *Second Testament*). Notice this: "through them," that is, through the knowledge of God's glorious promises, believers, in yet another grace, "may participate in the divine nature" itself! Participation points us all at a mutual indwelling and communion with Jesus Christ—with one another. Participation in the divine nature empowers believers to yet one more grace, namely, to flee "the decay in desire in the Kosmos" (1:4, *Second Testament*).

There is something utterly profound and unlike anything else in the New Testament in what I have just sketched. What Paul describes as being "in Christ" Peter intensifies and elevates to, and I now paraphrase in more graphic language, Christians *becoming partners, or common-life participants, in the divine nature*. The boundaries between the divine and the human, between Jesus Christ and us, are crossed in a mutual indwelling: Christ in us, we in Christ. But this in-Christ-ness is the very nature of God, what makes God God. God in us, we in God. While many would claim the union described here does not occur until the final kingdom, it would be a mistake to think we can't begin to experience this union in the here and now.

In fact, we can describe our participation in the divine nature by looking at relationships. The more we love and adore someone, and the more that someone returns love and adoration to us, the more we become like them. We can over time indwell one another relationally. We can say that devoted love to someone we love mimics, or at least attempts to mimic, this mutual indwelling. My wife Kris and I cannot do or say or think without the one knowing what the other is about to do or say because the other is thinking what we think they are thinking! All our good loves participate in God's love. The difference is that God is absolute, and we are finite; and the indwelling of God is Father, Son, and Spirit while our indwelling is with other humans and with God, a finite being with a finite being, or a finite being with the Infinite One. We indwell God or God indwells us because we are in Christ, who perfectly and infinitely indwells the Father (and the Spirit). The grace of participation in the divine nature in Christ works transformation in us.

That location in union with Christ is the "divine power" in us that provides "everything we need for a godly life" (1:3), and here Peter uses a term quite common in 1 Timothy. The Greek term *eusebeia*, like the Latin term *pietas*, points at a public religious life that is socially respectable. An important study of these terms by T. Christopher Hoklotubbe translates the term "civilized piety," which I have used in *The Second Testament*. I connect this term in 2 Peter with the emphasis on doing good in 1 Peter (2:14, 15, 20; 3:6, 17; 4:19). We won't get far from redemptive knowledge in 2 Peter. This grace of divine power at work in us to for a "godly life" comes to us "through our knowledge" of God. Inside that redemptive knowledge are the divine promises that empower participation and union with Christ, which empowers us to flee from this world's corruptions.

CHRISTIAN VIRTUES

Now we can see why Christian destiny and graces are so important for Christian virtues: without them there is no human capacity to live out Christian virtues. The virtues Peter lists are not so much an assembly line of *first master this and then move on to the next virtue to master*. Rather, they are the overflow of a character being transformed by the graces we just sketched. Twice Peter calls attention to the agency of a believer, and the term he uses evokes serious commitment (1:5, 10). The NIV has "make every effort," and *The Second Testament* has "having brough all seriousness, supply" and "seriously commit." Peter evokes the person who is all-in, devoted, concentrated, and has lost the distractions of peripheral vision. At 1:10–11 Peter urges them to "confirm" the work God has done in their life, and in 1:9 he reminds that they have been "cleansed from their past sins."

The virtues begin with faith, a term used but twice in this letter (1:1, 5). Faith is a gift (1:1), is directed at God in Christ, and the promises of Christian destiny. Faith is sometimes perceived as an act of the will, but Catherine González warns us about the mystery of even our personal faith—how it happened, why it happened, even when it happened. She writes, "Faith simply happens. It is an experience, however gradual or sudden. We find we have faith whereas earlier we did not. Acts of the will are involved. . . . The reality, however, is a mystery. We know that we cannot simply will ourselves to have faith. It must be an experience and not simply an intellectual decision. God's grace is involved. The work of the Holy Spirit is necessary. At the same time, faith often develops slowly, through a long process in which we know we could have turned away any number of times along the way." And she adds this, with which I agree completely:

"We probably interpret our experience of faith according to the theological tradition in which we stand" (González, *2 Peter*, 165–66).

But faith is the beginning, not the end. David deSilva once described faith as an evacuation (from the world) in these terms: "salvation isn't just a matter of an isolated decision. It's a matter of following an evacuation route. Decision is important, but it has to be a decision to follow the evacuation route, because salvation—safety—lies at the *end* of an evacuation route, not at its beginning" (deSilva, *In Season and Out*, 210).

The person who lives in light of the Christian destiny drawing upon the graces of Christian virtues, will add to her faith the following virtues. These don't happen all at once or once and for all. These are symptoms of a person who lives in light of the destiny on the basis of the graces, and those graces make for a person who lives a publicly respectable life.

Faith
    Goodness
        Knowledge
            Self-control
                Perseverance
                    Godliness
                        Sibling-love
                            Love

One can compare these to the Beatitudes of Matthew 5:1–12, with the fruit of the Spirit in Galatians 5:22–23, with the virtues of Romans 5:3–5, as well as with the character of an overseer in 1 Timothy 3:1–7. They overlap yet they are not the same, and that's because there's no insider secret for how to obtain the virtues or to some one-and-only-one list of virtues. The link from one virtue to the next finds its finale or apex in love, with the suggestion that all virtues find their ultimacy in love of God, love of self, and love of others. The promise Peter makes deserves notice. Those on this path of forming into love will prevent their becoming either "workless" and "fruitless" (1:8, *Second Testament*).

This list, along with the Beatitudes and the fruit of the Spirit, can be compared with this list of virtues from the Dead Sea Scrolls:

> Upon earth their operations are these: one enlightens a man's mind, making straight before him the paths of true righteousness and causing his heart to fear the laws of God. This spirit engenders humility, patience, abundant compassion, perpetual goodness, insight, understanding, and powerful wisdom resonating to each of God's deeds, sustained by His constant faithfulness. It engenders a spirit knowledgeable in every plan of action, zealous for the laws of righteousness, holy in its thoughts, and steadfast in purpose. This spirit encourages plenteous compassion upon all who hold fast to truth, and glorious purity combined with visceral hatred of impurity in its every guise. It results in humble deportment allied with a general discernment, concealing the truth, that is, the mysteries of knowledge. To these ends is the earthly counsel of the spirit to those whose nature yearns for truth. Through a gracious visitation all who walk in this spirit will know healing, bountiful peace, long life, and multiple progeny, followed by eternal blessings and perpetual joy through life everlasting. They will receive a crown of glory with a robe of honor, resplendent forever and ever. (1QS 4:4–8, translation Wise, Abegg, Cook)

QUESTIONS FOR REFLECTION AND APPLICATION

1. How does privilege impact our ability and desire to focus on the here and now of life instead of focusing on future life in heaven?

2. What does it mean to participate in divine nature?

3. How does divine power equip humans to live a godly life?

4. Do you have any close human relationships with a "mutual indwelling" component? What is that like, and how could aspects of that relationship model to you the kind of relationship possible with Jesus?

5. Consider deSilva's idea of faith as an evacuation route to salvation. If faith is making the ongoing decisions to stay on the route, how does that differ from a "sinner's prayer" type of salvation?

FOR FURTHER READING

David deSilva, *In Season and Out: Sermons for the Christian Year* (Bellingham, Washington: Lexham, 2019).

T. Christopher Hoklotubbe, *Civilized Piety: The Rhetoric of* Pietas *in the Pastoral Epistles and the Roman Empire* (Waco, Texas: Baylor University Press, 2017).

M.O. Wise, M. Abegg, E.M. Cook, *The Dead Sea Scrolls: A New Translation* (rev. ed.; New York: HarperCollins, 2005).

ESTABLISHING
THE FAITH

2 Peter 1:12–21

^{12} *So I will always remind you of these things, even though you know them and are firmly established in the truth you now have.* ^{13} *I think it is right to refresh your memory as long as I live in the tent of this body,* ^{14} *because I know that I will soon put it aside, as our Lord Jesus Christ has made clear to me.* ^{15} *And I will make every effort to see that after my departure you will always be able to remember these things.*

^{16} *For we did not follow cleverly devised stories when we told you about the coming of our Lord Jesus Christ in power, but we were eyewitnesses of his majesty.* ^{17} *He received honor and glory from God the Father when the voice came to him from the Majestic Glory, saying, "This is my Son, whom I love; with him I am well pleased."* ^{18} *We ourselves heard this voice that came from heaven when we were with him on the sacred mountain.*

^{19} *We also have the prophetic message as something completely reliable, and you will do well to pay attention to it, as to a light shining in a dark place, until the day dawns and the morning star rises in your hearts.* ^{20} *Above all, you must understand that no prophecy of Scripture came about by the prophet's own interpretation of things.* [21] *For prophecy never had its origin in the human will, but prophets, though human, spoke from God as they were carried along by the Holy Spirit.*

E very generation of parents, of teachers, of pastors, and of youth leaders cares immensely about how to pass the faith on to the next generation. Kara Powell and Chap Clark probe how to form "sticky faith" (*Sticky Faith*) while Kenda Creasy Dean, in her book *Almost Christian*, explores the same concern form the ground up. How to ensure that the current generation—the present set of children in our care, or the church folks we worship with each Sunday—are established in the faith? How to respond to the manifold accusations against the truth of Christian claims about Jesus? Peter, clearly concerned about firming up the believers, chooses to "remind" and "refresh" believers (1:12, 13), and in doing both he refutes the accusations. Peter faced accusations that the Parousia, commonly referred to as the Second Coming or the Return of Christ, was a myth, and that the prophecies of Israel had no divine origins. His responses can be summarized: Since God inspired Scripture, since Jesus was transfigured before their eyes, and since Peter and others were witnesses of the transfiguration, the prediction of Jesus's return is secure.

Peter establishes the faith and reliability of prophecies from three angles: tradition, experience, and Scripture. You have perhaps heard of the "Wesleyan Quadrilateral." This expression refers to the four elements that formed the foundation of the Methodist or Wesleyan teaching and theology: Scripture, which is first; then tradition, reason, and Christian experience (Thorsen, *Wesleyan Quadrilateral*). Today's passage explicitly makes use of three (tradition, experience, Scripture). Reason is not mentioned but any reading of the letter demonstrates Peter is reasoning his way along with his readers. However, this eager foursome are not equals. Scripture, or in today's passage, "the prophetic message," is first (*prima scriptura*), and the cover to Thorsen's book charts the path that begins with Scripture. This path is the wise path of the church. It is not the whole solution to the challenge, but it is the heart.

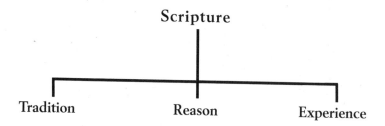

TRADITION

Peter reminds and refreshes the believers "even though you know them and are firmly established in the truth you now have," or one could translate "the present truth" (1:12; quoting NIV then *Second Testament*). So well formed are they in the Christian tradition's grasp of the gospel that Peter only wants to "refresh [their] memory" (1:13). The word behind "refresh" can be translated with "raise you up" or even "awaken." Teachers tapping into memories revive old memories and beliefs, so they become a living presence. Since Peter knows he's about to die he wants to leave a deposit they will never be able to forget (1:15). You may wonder, and I do, too, if Peter thought he would actually be present in some way by handing on his teaching in a memorable form. Most think he's pointing them to this letter, though I like the view held by fewer that he is pointing them at the Gospel of Mark, which early Christian tradition stated was first orally spoken by Peter and Mark wrote it down. Here is what the first major church historian wrote about Peter and Mark:

> When Peter had publicly preached the Logos in Rome and spoke in the Gospel by means of the Spirit, those who were present, being many, asked Mark to record what Peter had said in writing, since Mark had accompanied him for a long way and had remembered his sayings. He did so, and gave the Gospel to those who requested it. When Peter learned of this, he neither prevented it nor encouraged it. (Clement, as reported by Eusebius, *History of the Church*, 6.14.6–7)

It would be hard to find a better instance of an apostle making "every effort" to leave a deposit of the gospel (1:15).

Too many churches today want to start all over again with Jesus, as if for the first time. Fresh starts are important, but you and I can only get back to Jesus by marching straight through twenty centuries of the Church. Just as we can't start all over with a new *Declaration of Independence* or a new *Constitution*. We can't because they formed us—the church's traditions and the founding American documents. Add to those formative documents the history of interpretation and tradition and we arrive at where we are. We can do no other. We are who we are because of our traditions. We might chuck some, but they are *in* us, and we are *in* them! To establish the faith, we need to awaken to the value of the hard-earned traditions of the Church. But I want to add something: the traditions are revived best by returning to Jesus all over again. Going back to Jesus, through the tradition because there's no other way, enlightens us to see (1) what in the tradition went astray and (2) what is not found in the tradition can become a fresh addition, and (3) what has gone silent in the tradition can be revived.

Experience

Peter's reminder hops into another lane when he turns to his own experience as a witness of the glorious Lord Jesus (1:16–18). That Peter turns here to the authenticity about the "coming of our Lord Jesus Christ in power" echoes Mark 9:1. What followed Mark 9:1 in Mark's Gospel was the transfiguration of Jesus, which is what Peter himself turns to in 2 Peter 1:16–18. Evidently the opponents of Peter, who will figure prominently in the next two chapters of this letter, scoffed and ridiculed Peter, the apostles, and believers for adhering to "cleverly devised stories" (NIV) or "enwisened myths" (*Second Testament*; 1:16). Peter assures believers their teachings were true to facts.

Peter was there, and he stretches for words that adequately paint the picture in his own memory. Notice his vocabulary: "majesty" and "honor and glory" coming out of heaven "from the Majestic Glory" and the classic words of both the baptism and transfiguration: "This is my Son, whom I love . . ." (1:17). Notice that Peter's memory is not a solo memory. He began verse sixteen with "we" and it was "we ourselves who heard this voice." That is, Peter with James and John.

To establish Christian faith in a family and in a community effectively means adhering to the identity-forming traditions of the Church universal (the great creeds, etc.) but also witnessing to the life of Jesus personally. Peter tells them about his own experience on that "sacred mountain." So, too, churches need voices that stand up and witness to their experiences with Jesus. We each know witnesses to Jesus who have formed us, and mine would be different than yours. Ours is to remember theirs as we continue theirs in telling our experiences with Jesus.

SCRIPTURE

Scripture for Peter certainly meant what we call the "Old Testament" even though he may have included stories about Jesus that would form into our four Gospels. Perhaps, too, he may have thought of some of Paul's letters, which he is about to mention, as part of what he means by "prophetic word" (1:19; *Second Testament*). He surely included prophecies about the second coming (1:16). His opponents probably argued that the prophecies of these early Christians were rooted in ancient Israel's prophecies, which themselves were untrue and unreliable myths and self-serving interpretations.

But Peter counters the opponents. Both Peter's memory and experience lead him to affirm the prophetic messages as "completely reliable" (NIV), which is a bit of an exaggerated translation. It means confirmed, valid, and firm. He urges them and us to "pay attention" or to absorb it, the one way receives light in dark room—and to do so until the ah-ha moments arrive.

What comes next can resolve a million misuses of the meaning of the word "prophecy." Prophecies are not the result of research, or study, and they are not "the prophet's own interpretation of things" (1:20). Prophecies have the following distinctive characteristics, and without each they are not prophecies:

1. They are from God.
2. They are spoken by human agents of God.
3. They are for the people of God.
4. They are empowered by the Holy Spirit.

For words to be prophetic means a person must claim they have heard from God; they have something for the people of God; their words are formed, shaped, and delivered under the power of the Spirit of God. At times you and I may experience something as prophetic when the person who uttered the word would never use that term for themselves.

Preaching an expository sermon is not prophecy. Writing a book based on research in the ancient world is not prophecy. Having a great idea is not prophecy. Reasoning your way to a solution to a problem is not prophecy. The gifts of preaching or teaching are not prophecy. A prophetic word is a gift given by God to a human to speak to the people of God as empowered by the Spirit of God. If you cannot say "This word for you people is from God" then you shouldn't call it prophecy. While some will say a prophetic word can be from one person to another, which I have myself received and given, the primary mode of prophecy in the Bible is a word from God through a prophet to the people of God. In other words, as a primary feature of prophecy is a message from God to the community of God.

Let's now return to what Peter has just claimed: the writings of the Old Testament, especially the words of the prophets, and the writings perhaps of Paul and the Gospel of Mark that was to be published, were for Peter prophetic word. Scripture, then, has a theology at work: Scripture is from God, through a human agent, for the people of God, and carried along by the Spirit of God—to penetrate hearts and minds today with God's message.

Closing

Peter has looked death in the eyes. He opens today's reading, writing about "tent of this body," "that I will soon put it aside, as our Lord Jesus Christ has made clear to me." His words are not unlike those who have had near-death experiences. A philosopher whose body had all but shut down completely wrote, "You never come back from elsewhere because elsewhere always comes back with you." That is, you can never undo that near-death experience as long as you live. He continues, "Once you 'experience' death, it shadows you like an uncanny double you cannot escape. The past decade has, in effect, been life *after* death for me. Contrary to expectation, the experience of dying without dying has been extraordinarily liberating. Living (with) death has allowed me to let go of the past and the future and to dwell in the present differently" (Taylor, *Last Works*, 121). I'm not saying Peter had a near-death experience, though the experience of Taylor reminds me of those I know who have been through such an experience. What I am saying is that Peter had faced death, knew his time was short, and he learned that his present was altogether different because of what he had learned. Because his time was short, he wanted to make the first things first in the memories of these believers.

QUESTIONS FOR REFLECTION AND APPLICATION

1. What role does Tradition play in this letter?

2. How does Experience function in this letter?

3. What does Scripture do in Peter's rhetoric?

4. Though Reason isn't explicit in this letter, how does Peter use or appeal to Reason?

5. Does your tradition value these four Wesleyan elements or different ones? Which element of a faith foundation is most important in your tradition?

FOR FURTHER READING

Clement, in Eusebius, *History of the Church: A New Translation*, trans. Jeremy M. Schott (Berkeley: University of California Press, 2019).

Kenda Creasy Dean, *Almost Christian: What the Faith of Our Teenagers Is Telling the American Church* (Oxford University Press, 2010).

Kara Powell and Chap Clark, *Sticky Faith: Everyday Ideas to Build Lasting Faith in Your Kids* (Grand Rapids: Zondervan, 2011).

Donald A.D. Thorsen, *The Wesleyan Quadrilateral: Scripture, Tradition, Reason & Experience as a Model of Evangelical Theology* (Lexington, Kentucky: Emeth Press, 2005).

THE CHURCH AND
FALSE TEACHERS

2 Peter 2:1–22

[1] *But there were also false prophets among the people, just as there will be false teachers among you. They will secretly introduce destructive heresies, even denying the sovereign Lord who bought them—bringing swift destruction on themselves.* [2] *Many will follow their depraved conduct and will bring the way of truth into disrepute.* [3] *In their greed these teachers will exploit you with fabricated stories. Their condemnation has long been hanging over them, and their destruction has not been sleeping.*

[4] *For if God did not spare angels when they sinned, but sent them to hell, putting them in chains of darkness to be held for judgment;*

[5] *if he did not spare the ancient world when he brought the flood on its ungodly people, but protected Noah, a preacher of righteousness, and seven others;*

[6] *if he condemned the cities of Sodom and Gomorrah by burning them to ashes, and made them an example of what is going to happen to the ungodly;*

[7] *and if he rescued Lot, a righteous man, who was distressed by the depraved conduct of the lawless* [8] *(for that righteous man, living among them day after day, was tormented in his righteous*

soul by the lawless deeds he saw and heard)—[9] if this is so, then the Lord knows how to rescue the godly from trials and to hold the unrighteous for punishment on the day of judgment. [10] This is especially true of those who follow the corrupt desire of the flesh and despise authority.

Bold and arrogant, they are not afraid to heap abuse on celestial beings; [11] yet even angels, although they are stronger and more powerful, do not heap abuse on such beings when bringing judgment on them from the Lord. [12] But these people blaspheme in matters they do not understand. They are like unreasoning animals, creatures of instinct, born only to be caught and destroyed, and like animals they too will perish.

[13] They will be paid back with harm for the harm they have done. Their idea of pleasure is to carouse in broad daylight. They are blots and blemishes, reveling in their pleasures while they feast with you. [14] With eyes full of adultery, they never stop sinning; they seduce the unstable; they are experts in greed—an accursed brood! [15] They have left the straight way and wandered off to follow the way of Balaam son of Bezer, who loved the wages of wickedness. [16] But he was rebuked for his wrongdoing by a donkey—an animal without speech—who spoke with a human voice and restrained the prophet's madness.

[17] These people are springs without water and mists driven by a storm. Blackest darkness is reserved for them. [18] For they mouth empty, boastful words and, by appealing to the lustful desires of the flesh, they entice people who are just escaping from those who live in error. [19] They promise them freedom, while they themselves are slaves of depravity—for "people are slaves to whatever has mastered them." [20] If they have escaped the corruption of the world by knowing our Lord and Savior Jesus Christ and are again entangled in it and are overcome, they are worse off at the end than they were at the beginning. [21] It would have been better for them not to have known the way of righteousness, than to have known it and then to turn their backs on the sacred command that

was passed on to them. ²² *Of them the proverbs are true: "A dog returns to its vomit," and, "A sow that is washed returns to her wallowing in the mud."*

A friend of a friend wrote me about a person in the church whose beliefs were way off. That person was evidently spreading those ideas and, after meeting with the leaders in the right way, he, Gollum-like, refused to budge an inch from his precious beliefs. From what I could see, the church handled the teachings as they should have. The church, however, opted for the strategy of totally shunning the man. Shunning creates emotional distance from the loving fellowship of the church (1 Corinthians 5:11). A more extreme form of shunning is excommunication, which is a more formal, institutional distancing and banning of a person from the church, its fellowship, and its sacraments. Heresy, or the teaching of what is contrary to the classical Creed (The Nicene Creed), or, in other churches, what is contrary to the church's vital confessional statements, has been a major cause of shunning and excommunication. The only legitimate reason for shunning, excommunication, or labeling someone a heretic is the protection of the people of God from the kinds of teaching that deny the gospel and so destroy a person's faith and split the church's fellowship. Peter brings up the latter at the very end of today's passage (2 Peter 2:20–21). And, finally, immoralities arise to the level of pastoral concerns and church holiness. So, ideas matter, but so do behaviors. Many would say bad behaviors emerge from bad beliefs, and good beliefs propagate good behaviors and—I'm a theologian after all—I want to agree with them. But don't we all know people who believe the right things and who abuse others? And sometimes those with funky ideas can be the most loving. So, simply ordering belief and behavior won't fit the facts.

Shunning, excommunication, and labeling someone with teaching heresy or practicing immorality should be the last resort. Genuine pastoral care for a person's bad ideas and behaviors begins in one-on-one conversations, in meetings with the pastoral leaders of a church, with others deemed potentially helpful, and only after those approaches have failed should the more formal acts be entertained. In all cases, the restoration of a person must be the direction of all conversations. In no cases should the issue be power, fragile egos, vendettas, vindication, or theological minutiae.

I don't know what Peter had done prior to writing this letter, nor do I know what local leaders had done with some of these false teachers who provoked today's passage. One strategy to restore a false teacher in the early church was prophet-like denunciation of false teaching and false prophecies and bad behaviors. I assume leaders had met with some of these false teachers and had gotten nowhere but into deeper trouble. Which leads to this: 2 Peter 2 is one side of a conversation. Jill Lepore, a historian and essayist, once wrote, "A one-sided correspondence is like a house without windows" (Lepore, *The Deadline*, 6). I would think Peter's strategy was a house with windows, that is, open communications. The church preserved this letter because the church from its earliest days experienced theological tomfoolery and worse (Acts 5:1–11; 8:9–25; and we see rebuttals of false teachings in nearly every book in the New Testament after Acts!).

Here is where we must focus every time:

1. the perceived problems must be demonstrably genuine problems,
2. the problems must be serious topics, and
3. the approach to the problem people must be guided by those with loving, pastoral care for the person or persons involved.

In today's passage, if you read carefully through 2 Peter 2:1–2 and 10b–19, you can map the errors and behaviors and problems at work—at least as they are put into words by Peter. The problems as presented are real and serious. So, we begin there.

THE PROBLEM PEOPLE

Bible studies best keep their noses in Scripture itself, and one of the secrets to Bible study is to let the Bible's own words guide our thinking. Here are Peter's words for the problem *people*: "false teachers," not unlike Israel's own "false prophets" (2:1). A false prophet is someone who claims to speak for God but isn't (Deuteronomy 18:20) or utters content out of line with God's will (Jeremiah 5:31). Catherine González writes about an unfortunate truth: "it would seem that every time God raises up true prophets, false ones arise as well" (González, *2 Peter*, 181). History proves her right.

THE PRESENTING PROBLEMS

The elaboration of the *presenting problems* generated by these problem people is best viewed in a list with no more commentary than necessary, and the verses include all the lines until the next Bible verse.

1. *Divide people against one another:* They will "secretly introduce destructive heresies [or "factions"]" (2:1).
2. *Confuse people about Christ:* They deny "the sovereign Lord who bought them."
3. *Seduce into immorality:* They will draw away believers into "depraved conduct" (2:2).

4. *Insult the truth:* They will "bring the way of truth into disrepute."

5. *Exploit the people:* Out of a "greed" for power, glory, or money they "exploit" believers "with fabricated words" (2:3; *Second Testament*). See also 2:14, where this greed can "seduce the unstable." In that context they are compared to the arrogant sin of Balaam who was rebuked by a donkey (2:15–16; cf. Numbers 22).

6. *Irreverent arrogance:* "Self-regarding bold ones!" So bold they "don't tremble at the splendors," which refers to the glorious ones, that is, to angels (2 Peter 2:10; *Second Testament*). Notice Jude 9.

7. *Blasphemers:* the term refers to verbal abuse of those with higher status, and in this case the abuse of angels (2:11).

8. *Beastly:* Peter degrades these false teachers by labeling them in a few ways as animals (2:12).

9. *Sensuality:* they want their "pleasure" all day long (2:13). Notably, Peter knows this happens in the presence of the believers: "while they feast with you" (2:13). Peter uses a potent pun: they have turned the *agape* feasts into *apatē* feasts (love feasts into deceit feasts).

10. *Adulterers* who "never stop sinning" (2:14), with their eyes constantly on the next dalliance. We can add "lustful desires" (2:18).

11. *Self-promoters and exaggerators* (2:18).

12. *Seducers of people:* this is probably the same as #1. They are divisive, factional tribalists. In seducing they promise freedom or liberation, probably from the stiffer ethical vision of the way of Jesus (2:19). The irony is that these false teachers are "slaves of depravity," which takes us back again to #3 and #9.

I'm struck, perhaps you are too, that no one would follow such persons. How, I continued to ask myself as I formed this list, would any believer fall for such a hideous way of life or those who teach such things? The answer is this: They wouldn't! Peter has exaggerated the truth about the false teachers because he wants the believers to know this way of life leads to the ultimate disaster. If someone comes into your church, or mine, wearing these twelve beliefs and behaviors, no one would be seduced into their way. It's a warning that exaggerations emerge from subtle and small beliefs and behaviors that eventually morph into much more serious problems.

Perhaps the saddest part of what Peter lists here is that some believers were falling for the false teachers, and Peter does not mince or tame or diminish the significance of abandoning the faith a person once adhered to: "they are worse off at the end than they were at the beginning" (2:20). He labels them as dogs and sows (2:22). This sounds a bit like a parabolic word of Jesus (Matthew 12:43–45).

Peter weaves into the entire chapter words about the consequences for those who follow the way of the false teachers:

1. Swift destruction (2:1).
2. Perish or "in their decay they will be decayed" (2:12; *Second Testament*).
3. Recompense for their "wrongdoing" (2:13; *Second Testament*).
4. Their future is the "blackest darkness" (2:17).

Peter's aim is not a nuanced, balanced description of the good and bad of the false teachers. No, he's exaggerated their shortcomings in order to distance the way of discipleship from the false teachers. At the same time as he distances them from the believers, he offers words to identify who the believers truly are. They are *not like the ways of the false teachers.* Their way of life is the opposite, and you might just go through each of the twelve marks above, along with the four expressions about the consequence, and flip the script into the way of Christ and the consequence for following Christ.

THE PASTORAL-PROPHETIC RESPONSE

So, what to do? First, like Peter and other prophet-like texts, we need to develop the skill of discernment. It is too easy to fall for the old, wearied, and rarely accurate slippery slope argument. That is, in seeing the least bit of variance in someone—they read a paraphrase Bible translation, they are amillennial, they've gone liturgical, they like to read someone "unapproved"—and pronouncing they'll deny Christ, become a sensualist, or start church divisions. Instead, we must develop a healthy perception of the gospel and of sound morality and learn to discern the current situation today with clear eyes. We can only do this by continual exposure to the Word of God as revealed by and in Christ, and by constant examination of the inner workings of our society and churches. I give a few crisp indicators of trouble in the making: the overuse of business models for the church that turn the church away from the Body of Christ to an organization and institution with policies and governance. The platforming of pastors and preachers on the basis of their so-called "charisma" and ability to draw a crowd that can put bills in the plate. The seduction of good church people away from routine spiritual formation in Bible reading, prayer, church fellowship, and mission. Seduced from those into whatever drives the energies of God's people today. The message of grace and salvation without the importance and requirement of discipleship, and many of the elements of the false teachers above are connected to this very problem: discipleship to Christ was disappearing.

Second, Peter pressed hard on the consequences of a disordered, misspent life. Many of us grew up with too much damnation and hellfire. (I heard sermons like this often as a child.) Many of us have turned away from the truth of final consequences (2:1, 12, 13, 17) and have lost the potency of learning to live before God and God's final approval. God's unconditional love includes not only the power of God to "rescue the godly from trials" (2:9) but also the warrant for those who choose to walk away from the way of Jesus Christ (2:20–22). A quick reading of 2:4–6, which reveals the judgment of God against angels, the ancient world in the time of Noah, and against Sodom and Gomorrah, sharpens Peter's argument because the believers have embraced the Scriptures. The God who rescues (cf. 1 Corinthians 10:13) is the same God who judges evil in order to establish the kingdom of God. Two things go hand-in-glove: a lack of discipleship fits easily with a diminishing of God's final judgment. Not because discipleship is motivated by fear or a threat, but because God is holy, God is righteous, and the God who rescues us rescues into a life of holiness and righteousness.

Many of us may wrinkle our foreheads or tilt our heads away from those verses, but they fit in the Bible's vision of a good God who loves us and wants what is best for us—even more than we want that best. There is no Bible without God's love, just as there is no Bible without consequences for turning from that loving God. In *The Great Divorce*, C.S. Lewis wrote words that ring truer today than they did in his day: "There are only two kinds of people in the end: those who say to God, 'Thy will be done,' and those to whom God says, in the end, 'Thy will be done.' All that are in Hell, choose it.

Without that self-choice there could be no Hell. No soul that seriously and constantly desires joy will ever miss it. Those who seek find. Those who knock it is opened" (Lewis, *Great Divorce*, 5).

QUESTIONS FOR REFLECTION AND APPLICATION

1. How do you think beliefs and behaviors interact in individual humans?

2. What kind of false or concerning beliefs have you heard people share in Christian circles? How were those beliefs handled by the pastors or leaders of those communities?

3. What is the possible impact on readers of Peter's exaggerated list of false teacher traits?

4. How might you develop more discernment that could help you see through false teachers and their teachings?

5. What is your perspective on final judgement and consequences for those who choose not to follow Jesus?

FOR FURTHER READING

C.S. Lewis, *The Great Divorce: A Dream* (New York: HarperOne, 2000).

Jill Lepore, *The Deadline: Essays* (New York: Liveright, 2023).

LIVING DURING THE DELAY

2 Peter 3:1–18

¹ Dear friends, this is now my second letter to you. I have written both of them as reminders to stimulate you to wholesome thinking. ² I want you to recall the words spoken in the past by the holy prophets and the command given by our Lord and Savior through your apostles.

³ Above all, you must understand that in the last days scoffers will come, scoffing and following their own evil desires. ⁴ They will say, "Where is this 'coming' he promised? Ever since our ancestors died, everything goes on as it has since the beginning of creation." ⁵ But they deliberately forget that long ago by God's word the heavens came into being and the earth was formed out of water and by water. ⁶ By these waters also the world of that time was deluged and destroyed. ⁷ By the same word the present heavens and earth are reserved for fire, being kept for the day of judgment and destruction of the ungodly.

⁸ But do not forget this one thing, dear friends: With the Lord a day is like a thousand years, and a thousand years are like a day. ⁹ The Lord is not slow in keeping his promise, as some understand slowness. Instead he is patient with you, not wanting anyone to perish, but everyone to come to repentance.

¹⁰ *But the day of the Lord will come like a thief. The heavens will disappear with a roar; the elements will be destroyed by fire, and the earth and everything done in it will be laid bare.*

¹¹ *Since everything will be destroyed in this way, what kind of people ought you to be? You ought to live holy and godly lives* ¹² *as you look forward to the day of God and speed its coming. That day will bring about the destruction of the heavens by fire, and the elements will melt in the heat.* ¹³ *But in keeping with his promise we are looking forward to a new heaven and a new earth, where righteousness dwells.*

¹⁴ *So then, dear friends, since you are looking forward to this, make every effort to be found spotless, blameless and at peace with him.* ¹⁵ *Bear in mind that our Lord's patience means salvation, just as our dear brother Paul also wrote you with the wisdom that God gave him.* ¹⁶ *He writes the same way in all his letters, speaking in them of these matters. His letters contain some things that are hard to understand, which ignorant and unstable people distort, as they do the other Scriptures, to their own destruction.*

¹⁷ *Therefore, dear friends, since you have been forewarned, be on your guard so that you may not be carried away by the error of the lawless and fall from your secure position.* ¹⁸ *But grow in the grace and knowledge of our Lord and Savior Jesus Christ. To him be glory both now and forever! Amen.*

When an author, a director, or a leader sorts out and sums up what they want you to hear in what they have said, you would do well to pay special attention. I recently wrote to an author of an internet article, and I asked, "Is your summary that your critics are not giving the whole story?" His answer was "Yes." That was his point. In Peter's second letter, which reminds me of Paul's second letter to Timothy (2 Timothy 1:6; 2:1–3, 8, 14; 3:1–9; 3:10—4:8), the apostle's point is to tie previous instructions to the second coming of Christ (3:1–18). This letter, and especially this last chapter of the letter, is a "reminder" that he hopes to "stimulate" the listeners to "wholesome thinking" or, as I have translated it, "raise up in memory your sincere mind" (3:1). That is, to toss sunlight into the room of their memory. Peter wants them to keep in mind "the words spoken in the past by the holy prophets," who again are Israel's prophets (see Isaiah 5:18–23; Jeremiah 5:12–7; Amos 9:9–10; Malachi 2:17) and maybe as well some early Christian prophets. They are to recall not just those prophets but also "the command" that the Lord Jesus gave to them "through your apostles" (3:2; see Mark 13).

Since the emphasis is clearly about those who ridicule the promise of the return of Christ, that is, those who scoff at the return because of the length of the delay, and since Peter will both explain what the "day" in "the Day of the Lord" means, and since he will sketch how to live as we await the return, we are on sure ground thinking both the prophets and the command of the Lord Jesus were about being prepared for the Parousia. The delay of the Parousia was a major issue in the early church. Today's passage instructs believers by providing a few approaches to the problem of the delay of the return of Christ. Take the long view, examine the meaning of words, realize the return will be sudden and surprising in its timing, and live now in light of that Day.

DELAY AND THE LONG VIEW

Many confess every Sunday in church the Nicene Creed, which contains this element of faith: "He will come again in glory to judge the living and the dead, and his kingdom will have no end." In fifty years I have heard a number of subtle scoffs about the second coming: that we should concentrate on life now instead of what happens after we die. The *Left Behind* series, which drew its strength from graphic books in the 60s and 70s, gets things so wrong we might as well give up on talking about eschatology. The New Testament authors, and even Jesus, seemed to think the Parousia would happen within a generation—and it's been 1990+ years since they said that—so we might as well drop that article of our faith. And, a once very popular view, the more one concentrates on the second coming the less one will be involved undoing this world's injustices. Today's scoffers join hands with first century scoffers. As Catherine González reminds us, "The coming judgment is an essential part of the gospel, however, and the behavior of Christians, those who acknowledge God's coming judgment, should be as moral as possible" (González, *Second Peter*, 192).

Those first century scoffers had an approach like the one just mentioned: "Ever since our ancestors died," and this must refer to the first generation of believers, "everything goes on as it has since the beginning of creation" (3:4). Peter responds by taking the long, long view. "Long ago by God's word the heavens came into being . . ." (3:5). As long, long ago God judged the world by a flood, so God will judge it again. This next time, however, God will judge not by water but by fire (3:6–7; cf. 3:10, 12). If it happened long ago, it could happen again—regardless of how long of a delay. If God created, God will judge—that's the core of Peter's long view. God creates by word and water; by water God judged the world; by word and fire God will judge the world.

Scoffers will often accompany those waiting. Peter, like Jude 18, has those who reject the truth of the gospel and the Parousia and live out a life that mocks those truths. Such persons, Peter says, not only mock this fundament of the Creed but they are "following their own evil desires" (2 Peter 3:3). As is so often the case in Peter's letters, what one believes and how one behaves are linked to one another. Click on the latter (erroneous ideas) and you get the former (distorted desires).

DELAY AND THE WORDVIEW

The operative word in need of a clear meaning is "day." When it comes to God a "day" is not a twenty-four-hour day. Thus, "with the Lord a *day* is like a thousand years" but also, noticing the exact opposite, "a thousand years is like a day" (3:8). The combination results in this: God is beyond, above, below, through, and in time. God relates to time, but time has no control on God. In particular, as one can see in Psalm 90:4, on which Peter's words are based, God dwells in infinite time and humans are connected now to finite time. Because of God's relationship to our sense of time, Peter urges the believers to recognize that "the Lord is not slow in keeping his promise" but instead is "patient" with humans (3:9). Peter could be echoing the prophet Habakkuk:

> For the revelation awaits an
>   appointed time;
>   it speaks of the end
>   and will not prove false.
> Though it linger, wait for it;
>   it will certainly come
>   and will not delay. (2:3)

The delay then does not point out some erroneous prediction. That would impugn God's character and truthfulness. Rather, the delay indicates the goodness of God in waiting for humans to respond to the truth of God. The time of our life privileges each of us to experience reality and turn to God. The goodness of God means God is "not wanting some to be destroyed but all to find space for conversion" (3:9; *Second Testament*).

DELAY AND THE SUDDEN VIEW

The patience of God is not endless. Suddenly, "like a thief," "the day of the Lord will come" (3:10). Peter picked this idea up from Jesus (Matthew 24:43; Luke 12:39) and perhaps heard about it with Paul, too (1 Thessalonians 5:1). John uses the image as well (Revelation 3:3; 16:15). Thieves, at least if they are not brazened, plan for a surreptitious strike. The return of the Lord will be just as unexpected, more surprising, and far more significant. Peter is not talking here about a rapture followed by a seven-year (according to one common interpretation) tribulation, which itself is followed by the Parousia. Peter speaks here only of the Parousia, commonly referred to as the Second Coming or the Return of Christ.

The suddenness or surprisingness of the Parousia forms one-half of Peter's instructions. As Larry George writes about when Jesus returns, "it will be like a thief (quick, quiet, and in secret) and will be chaotic and catastrophic, with an end time prophetic description of the destruction and annihilation of heavenly and celestial bodies. All on earth will be judged and destroyed" (George, "2 Peter," 493).

The grave consequences of divine judgment entail a purgation of this world that involves its being burned up and recreated into a "new heaven and new earth" (2 Peter 3:10, 12–13). Such a metaphor-dense vision of what God will do can overwhelm some of us, but its intent is, literally, to put the fear of God in our hearts. As we previously cited the Creed, so we can remind ourselves of the tradition of the church: God will judge the living and the dead, and the final kingdom will be life for those who survive divine scrutiny. God is good, God loves us, and God is patient. But God is holy, God is just, and God will judge. It is foolish and reckless to ignore these truths.

Some observe that Peter's terms here sound like the Stoic philosophers of the first century, and they could be accurate. Peter as a pastor may well have adapted to the audience's context, but Pheme Perkins, who knows her Stoicism well, raises a bit of a red flag when she writes "Biblical eschatology cannot be turned into ancient Stoic or even modern cosmology because the fate of the universe expresses divine judgement" (Perkins, *Second Peter*, 191).

DELAY AND THE DAILY VIEW

The irony of those who think concentrating too much on the return of Christ leads to inactivity in this world is that Jesus, Paul, Peter, and John believed the exact opposite. Peter's theory turns the future hope into a motivation for transformed life now. The delay of the Parousia for him means a new view of the daily life of the believer. Here is what it looks like for them and for us: it begins with a wonderful question that feels like it goes on and on with a sidebar to boot: "*So what kind of persons is it necessary for you to be* in devoted behavior and civilized piety, anticipating and hurrying the Parousia of God's Day (because of which the heavens set on fire will be loosened and the first categories, burning up, melt)?" (3:11–12; *Second Testament*). (I italicized here the central terms of this question.)

The question is about the kind of life one lives. Peter's terms, echoing the theme of doing good in 1 Peter, are about behaviors (cf. 1:5–9): "devoted [or holy] behavior" and "civilized piety." In their holiness and publicly respectable life they have the opportunity—read this slowly—to hurry the Parousia of God's Day! The NIV has "speed its coming." While one side of that Day is judgment, the other side is new creation—"A new heavens and a new earth"—"In which rightness resides" (3:13; *Second Testament*). What those with

177

a morally formed conscience and character most want is a world in which what is right is done and what is wrong is gone. What does this kind of life look like in other particulars? Peter mentions these: by God's grace in the new creation humans will be spotless, blameless, and at peace with God *and therefore they are now* to form a life that approaches spotlessness, blamelessness, and peacefulness (3:14). Down in verse seventeen he resumes with "be on your guard" and "grow in the grace and knowledge of our Lord and Savior Jesus Christ." I like this emphasis: growth in grace is more than theological expertise. It is growth in the kind of grace that God reveals to us in a person, Jesus Christ. Growing in grace is about knowing Jesus more and more.

Time now reveals that God is patient, and when Peter mentions this, he connects God's patience with God's salvation with the apostle Paul himself. Which leads to one of the most uttered statements in Bible classrooms: Paul spoke "with the wisdom God gave him" but, truth be told even for a fellow apostle, "his letters contain some things that are hard to understand." Peter connects Paul's letter to "Scriptures" in 3:16, so his respect for Paul reaches the heights. Yet, he knows how hard it is to comprehend some of Paul's theology. Peter just has to be talking about Romans 7 if not also Romans 9–11! Perhaps, however, he's talking about the law, because some think Paul has erased it from history for church folks. Some "unstable people distort" what Paul wrote. He wrote Galatians and Romans to rebut what some had said, and surely James 2:14–26 is responding either to those who distorted Paul or even to Paul himself. Notice that Peter mentions "law" in "lawless" in verse seventeen. Perhaps also we need to consider the false teachers to be perverting what Paul taught about the Parousia. After all, that's been Peter's concern in both his second and third chapters. He wants his churches to be "forewarned" so they will not fall for the "error of the lawless" and thus, sadly and tragically, "fall from your secure position" (3:17; cf. 1:8–11; 2:1–3, 20).

Peter turns the lock on this letter with a benediction about Jesus Christ, one that can be uttered in Peter's daily life. Jesus forms the heart and center of Peter's universe and knows now and forever Jesus is deserving of the "glory."

That great preacher, Fred Craddock, coming to the end of this letter said "At one point, he [the author of 2 Peter] goes into a valedictory, a sordid deathbed speech. . . . And he gathers the church around the foot of the bed. That's very impressive, the last words of the old writer. At other times he gets up on his hind legs and just screams bad names at the opposition, a lot of name calling. What has him so exercised?" (Craddock, *Collected Sermons*, 281). We can now answer that question: the false teachers are corrupting the gospel by denying the Parousia of Jesus Christ, and Peter will have none of it. We may be too comfortable lounging on our couches to recognize that at times we too might need to get up with Peter on our own hind legs! Craddock ended that sermon with a prayer, and it spoke to me so I'm putting right here for my ending, too, or perhaps for a new beginning—you be the judge.

Gracious God, sometimes how stale, flat and taste-less seem all the uses of this present world. It seems we gather to rehearse what never happens. We scatter to address the inhumanity in the world only to find ourselves like children with teaspoons standing before an ocean. There needs to be an end to things. There needs to be a beginning to things. And yet we grieve over endings and were afraid of beginnings. O God, be the Alpha and the Omega of our lives and the life of the world for the sake of Christ. Amen. (Craddock, *Collected Sermons*, 287)

QUESTIONS FOR REFLECTION AND APPLICATION

1. Considering the delay of Jesus' return (the Parousia) as a major concern for Peter's audience, how does that make sense of how he concludes this letter?

2. What is your perspective on the second coming of Jesus?

3. How would you respond to people who argue, "Concentrating too much on the return of Christ leads to inactivity in this world"?

4. How might it affect the way you live each day to remind yourself more often that Jesus will be returning at an unexpected time?

5. As you conclude your study of Peter's letters, what are the key takeaways you learned?

FOR FURTHER READING

Fred B. Craddock, *The Collected Sermons of Fred B. Craddock* (Louisville: Westminster John Knox, 2011).

JUDE

THE PEOPLE
OF JESUS

Jude 1–2

¹ Jude, a servant of Jesus Christ and a brother of James,
To those who have been called, who are loved in God the Father and kept for Jesus Christ:
² Mercy, peace and love be yours in abundance.

What do you call those who are in the church? Or who are followers of Jesus? The apostle Paul's favorite term (by far) was "siblings" or as the NIV has it, "brothers and sisters." Peter's first letter dubbed them "foreigners and exiles" (1:1; 2:11). His second letter called them believers (1:1, 5). First, what does Jude call himself? Not only does Jude dub himself a "slave" of Jesus (Jude 1; *Second Testament*) and a "brother" of James (1), Jude pulls from his thesaurus three significant terms for the people of God who follow Jesus. Jude could be translated Youdas or Youda or Judah, while James comes from Yakōbos, which would be Jacob, but later languages adapted it to James. The traditional reason for Jude connecting himself to James is because they are both brothers of Jesus. Which makes for something on the order of a

Jesus-family dynasty in the early church (Mark 6:3). Now to Jude's terms for the church.

The people of Jesus are *called* (1). Let's turn to another author first. Paul was "called" to be an apostle (Romans 1:1) but more important are those "called to belong to Jesus Christ" (1:6, 7), who are themselves all called to be conformed to the image of Christ (8:28). Only a couple other passages are like these (1 Corinthians 1:1, 2, 24). Jude, then, uses a relatively uncommon term for the people of God, and this term evokes a major term in the Old Testament: Israel was called, that is, they were elected by God. The Greek term for "called" is *klētos* and for "elect ones" it is *eklektos*, a term used by Peter in his first letter (1:1; 2:4, 6, 9). The experience of God's grace that draws a person into relationship with Christ evokes a sense of election, of being called. Something happens to us from outside ourselves. Theologians would later develop a much more comprehensive sense of the doctrine of election, but the harshness of some of the later presentations created rifts in the church. Recent studies have used texts like John 15:16 where Jesus' calling and election are "so that you might go and bear fruit." That is, election cannot be reduced to who's in and who's out. Election transforms us into agents of mission.

The emphasis of Jude is not on being called but on being *loved*. Jude frames God's love for the people of Jesus in two ways. First, they are *loved in God the Father* (1), and so become God's *loved ones* (3, 17, 20). God's love for God's people is an affective (deep in emotion), rugged commitment that takes shape as a covenant between God and his people (Genesis 12; 15; 17; 22; Exodus 19–24). God's covenant involves divine presence in a variety of shapes, like God's presence in the temple or in the Holy Spirit or in Jesus as "God with us" (Matthew 1:23), and that covenant engages the people of God being transformed into what God wants of those people.

Now his third term for the church. The people of Jesus are *kept for Jesus Christ* (1). Jude wants the called-and-loved ones to know that God guards them until they can be reunited again or united for the first time with Jesus at his Parousia. Jude tightens the term "kept," *tēreō*, by putting it in the perfect passive tense. That is, it could be translated with "who have been and are kept and will be kept" for that Day. Peter uses this term for the inheritance (1 Peter 1:4) but also for those who are guarded until the judgment (2 Peter 2:4, 9, 17; 3:7), and Jude uses the term as it is found in 2 Peter at Jude 6 and Jude 13, while at Jude 21 he summons the called-and-loved ones to "keep yourselves in God's love."

QUESTIONS FOR REFLECTION AND APPLICATION

1. Consider what it was like for two of Jesus' brothers to be leaders in the early church. What do you imagine about their lives and experiences?

2. What does it mean for the people of God to be called?

3. How does calling connect with election?

4. If God's love is emotional, as suggested in this lesson, how is that different for you than God's love being merely a commitment?

5. How does it feel for you to know you are called, loved, and kept by God?

THE PROBLEM
PEOPLE

Jude 3–16

3 Dear friends, although I was very eager to write to you about the salvation we share, I felt compelled to write and urge you to contend for the faith that was once for all entrusted to God's holy people. 4 For certain individuals whose condemnation was written about long ago have secretly slipped in among you. They are ungodly people, who pervert the grace of our God into a license for immorality and deny Jesus Christ our only Sovereign and Lord.

5 Though you already know all this, I want to remind you that the Lord at one time delivered his people out of Egypt, but later destroyed those who did not believe. 6 And the angels who did not keep their positions of authority but abandoned their proper dwelling—these he has kept in darkness, bound with everlasting chains for judgment on the great Day. 7 In a similar way, Sodom and Gomorrah and the surrounding towns gave themselves up to sexual immorality and perversion. They serve as an example of those who suffer the punishment of eternal fire.

8 In the very same way, on the strength of their dreams these ungodly people pollute their own bodies, reject authority and heap abuse on celestial beings. 9 But even the archangel Michael, when

he was disputing with the devil about the body of Moses, did not himself dare to condemn him for slander but said, "The Lord rebuke you!" 10 Yet these people slander whatever they do not understand, and the very things they do understand by instinct—as irrational animals do—will destroy them.

11 Woe to them! They have taken the way of Cain; they have rushed for profit into Balaam's error; they have been destroyed in Korah's rebellion.

12 These people are blemishes at your love feasts, eating with you without the slightest qualm—shepherds who feed only themselves. They are clouds without rain, blown along by the wind; autumn trees, without fruit and uprooted—twice dead. 13 They are wild waves of the sea, foaming up their shame; wandering stars, for whom blackest darkness has been reserved forever.

14 Enoch, the seventh from Adam, prophesied about them: "See, the Lord is coming with thousands upon thousands of his holy ones 15 to judge everyone, and to convict all of them of all the ungodly acts they have committed in their ungodliness, and of all the defiant words ungodly sinners have spoken against him." 16 These people are grumblers and faultfinders; they follow their own evil desires; they boast about themselves and flatter others for their own advantage.

In Peter's second chapter of his second letter (see pp. 160–162), we observed twelve presenting problems of the problem people that Peter needed to address. Many today think Peter borrowed language from Jude 3–16. That is the best explanation for the relationship of these two letters: Peter made use of Jude. As there, so here: we need to map the problems Jude was discovering among the called-and-loved ones to whom he wrote this letter. His observations are found in verses 4, 8–10, 12–13, 16, and 17–18. Add to these the past examples or models of misbehaving people of God, which are found in verses 5–7 and 11.

PRESENT PROBLEM PEOPLE

It's quite an assortment of denigrating terms for those who violate the covenant love of God with rebellion, sin, and disobedience. If these terms add up to observable behaviors, it would not have been difficult for the called-and-loved ones to recognize the problem people. Their furtive ways must recall how they weaseled their way into the inner fabric of the followers of Jesus.

Verse 4:
1. Secretive in behaviors
2. Ungodly or impious
3. Flaunters of sensualities
4. Deniers of Jesus Christ

Verse 8:
5. Visionary experiences
6. Pollute their own bodies
7. Reject authority
8. Insult or slander angelic beings

Verse 10:
9. Insult or slander out of ignorance
10. As irrational animals their instincts degrade them

Verse 11:
11. Connected to the wrong examples: Cain, Balaam, Korah

Verse 12:
12. Blemishes at your love feasts
13. Self-absorbed pastors
14. Dead

Verse 13:
15. Shameful
16. Wandering into final darkness

Verse 16:
>   17. Hyper critics
>   18. Sensuous for evil (and also v. 18)
>   19. Self-promoters
>   20. Flatterers
>
> Verse 18:
>   21. Scoffers
>
> Verse 19:
>   22. Divisive
>   23. Lack the Holy Spirit

If anyone has gotten to this page in the New Testament is still captured by the idea that the earliest churches were pure and godly and loving and generous and laced up, tied, and even zippered with goodness, this little letter ought to dispel the idea into the mists of idealism. With a traditional dating of the book in the 60s or so, it took about a generation for the church to attract and get polluted by such problem people. In other datings, it took only two or three generations. With either dating the realities we learn from the New Testament establish that the church was only pure for about a day! (And that's generous.) The problem with the church is the people, and the people I'm talking about are sinners. Each and every one of them and us.

I want to draw attention to only a few characteristics of the problem people in Jude's view. First, "these ungodly people" (8; cf. 10, 12, 16, 19) are integrated into the church people. They are "blemishes at your love feasts" (12), which were meals connected to the Lord's Supper. Second, even more they are "shepherds who feed only themselves" (12). That is, they are leaders in the local church. Third, their denial of Jesus Christ (4) is most likely not an overt refusal to "say the Creed" nor explicit teachings against standard Christian beliefs about Jesus. Their denial is a general disposition that opposes the way of Jesus. Fourth, they probably appeal to their authority on the basis of their visionary experiences (8; like Colossians 2:18), which leads them to reject other authorities, including an audacious insulting of the "archangel Michael," and to become hyper critics, self-promoters, and flatterers (16). As such, they become divisive (19). Finally, these ungodly leaders flaunt their sensualities that from a biblical perspective pollute the body (4, 8, 16, 18). Jude's ultimate labels for these people is that they are ungodly, are in the line of Cain (the archetypal sinner) and Balaam (the mercenary prophet) and Korah (antinomian heretic), are dead, and they lack the Spirit. Yet, because of their skills in accessing the church folks in a furtive manner, they are both present and influential in the churches to which Jude writes.

Noticeably, Jude quotes from the apocalypse of *1 Enoch* in Jude 14–15. One of my professors once said *1 Enoch* was the *Late, Great Planet Earth* of its day. Whether true or not, the apocalypse was so influential Jude could quote it with some sense of its authority for his argument. When Jude wrote, there was no "canon" as we know it today. The canon of Scripture, though I believe God led the church to the New and Old Testament's books, remains a consensus of the church. Any study of it reveals that some books were immediate consensus while others were not so immediate. What the study reveals, too, is that some thought some other books ought to be given a voice. Perhaps, and I say this only as a perhaps, Jude thought *1 Enoch* deserved a voice at the table.

PAST PROBLEM PEOPLE

In the heart of today's passage, Jude pulls from Scripture three connections to the present problem people and makes use of the term "example" or model (5–7). Everyone seems to have a ne'er-do-well in the family, but Jude's examples pull out more than ne'er-do-wells from Israel's stories. He finds an example of those whose faith fell apart (5), angels who through rebellion "abandoned their proper dwelling" (6), and the sensualities of Sodom and Gomorrah (7). To these he will add three more: "the way of Cain . . . Balaam's error . . . Korah's rebellion" (11). By the way, there was endless speculation about the angels of Genesis 6, leading to the very influential apocalyptic text *1 Enoch*, and an echo of that speculation can be found in 1 Peter 3:19–20.

Jude concentrates the gravity of these examples on the consequences of their sins: the children of Israel were destroyed, the angels have been imprisoned in darkness, and by implication the cities were devastated. Jude's concentration leads him to the implications for the ungodly leaders in their midst. They become "an example of those who suffer the punishment of eternal fire" (7). The rhetorical impact for Jude flies in two directions: at the ungodly, his words warn them of what could happen to them if they don't repent, and at the called-and-loved, his words serve to "contend for the faith" and to "keep you from stumbling" so they can be presented "before his glorious throne without fault and with great joy" (24).

PROBLEM PEOPLE TODAY

Texts like these can make us way too suspicious of other people. Yes, but also the same texts can make us far too naïve about influential voices among us. Jude's image for us comes from the world of athletics. In verse three he urges them to "wage a contest for the faith" (*Second Testament*). In verse five he expresses that they are established and well-formed in the faith, writing that they "already know all this." The image speaks of discipline, effort, competition, and even defeats leading to more demanding preparations and training sessions. All in all, athletics takes the courage to risk your efforts against the competition. The contest is about preservation and faithfulness to the "faith that was once and for all entrusted to God's holy people" (3). That faith has experienced challenges from opponents from day one. Christian teachers have the responsibility to know the faith and to preserve that faith in the heat of competition against that faith. When I think of those who have waged the contest, I think of Alister McGrath, Dallas Willard, and Craig Keener, who is a one-man argument for the integrity of miracles. I also think of Beth Barr, who has dug her heels in to defend the gifting of women; of Kristin Kobes DuMez, who has called out masculinism in high places; and I think of both Robert Chao Romero and Jemar Tisby, who have constructed a considerable platform to fight racism and white supremacy. Each of these has waged a contest for the faith.

A common name for problem people in churches today is *narcissist*: a person with an unusual sense of their greatness, a fragile ego, and a lack of empathy for others, all of which lead them to find people who will surround them with affirmation. Hints of such a personality type can be found in the twenty-three characteristics above. Another name today is someone who is spiritually abusive, which boils down to bad character abusing positional or relational power. There are three basic elements to spiritual abuse: (1) the asymmetry in power between a person with some kind of spiritual authority and another person; (2) it is most noticeable when there is a *pattern* of abuse, though a single case can constitute spiritual abuse, and at times spiritual abuse penetrates a culture so much it becomes systemic; (3) and behaviors by that spiritual authority that psychologically, emotionally, and spiritually wound a person. Again, hints of spiritual abuse come through some of the twenty-three traits. To turn toward modern labels like narcissist or abuser leads us away from a rigid use of the traits in Jude to more synthetic, comprehensive patterns of church infections.

What can you do about problem people in the church? First, and above all, soak yourself in Scripture and prayer, invoking the Spirit's guidance about what to do. Second, rely on your church's or institution's policies of reporting or whistleblowing. Most of these will instruct a person to speak directly to the person about whom they have a concern. Sometimes this is the way of wisdom, and other times it is unsafe and potentially harmful. Third, ensure that you are healthy enough to endure what often turns into pushbacks, gaslighting, sealioning, and even sidelining and silencing and shunning. Fourth, acquire in advance a solid support group. Fifth, if you confront a person, have someone with you as an advocate. An advocate is not there to be the judge but to listen, witness what happens, take note, and to support you. Sixth, give yourself realistic expectations. Which means, don't expect the person to fall on their knees in humility, confession, lament, repentance, and transformation. The most important expectation is to be heard, whether any change occurs or not. Finally, I recommend giving yourself a timetable that puts into order how long you can wait with how much you can endure (McKnight, Barringer, *Pivot*).

QUESTIONS FOR REFLECTION AND APPLICATION

1. How do Jude's notations on problem people impact your impression of the early church?

2. Have you ever seen people call themselves Christians and hold standard Christian beliefs yet live with a disposition opposed to the way of Jesus?

3. How do modern words like "narcissist" and "abuser" help you contextualize Jude's warnings about problem people into your church today?

4. How does Jude's list of the behaviors of problem people help you spot red flags of unsafe people in your life?

5. When have you experienced challenges and defeats that have inspired you to train harder and try again? How can that experience inspire you in your spiritual life?

FOR FURTHER READING

Scot McKnight and Laura Barringer, *Pivot: The Priorities, Practices, and Powers that can Transform your Church into a Tov Culture* (Carol Stream: Tyndale Elevate, 2023).

WHAT TO DO?

Jude 17–25

[17] *But, dear friends, remember what the apostles of our Lord Jesus Christ foretold.* [18] *They said to you, "In the last times there will be scoffers who will follow their own ungodly desires."* [19] *These are the people who divide you, who follow mere natural instincts and do not have the Spirit.*

[20] *But you, dear friends, by building yourselves up in your most holy faith and praying in the Holy Spirit,* [21] *keep yourselves in God's love as you wait for the mercy of our Lord Jesus Christ to bring you to eternal life.*

[22] *Be merciful to those who doubt;* [23] *save others by snatching them from the fire; to others show mercy, mixed with fear—hating even the clothing stained by corrupted flesh.*

[24] *To him who is able to keep you from stumbling and to present you before his glorious presence without fault and with great joy—* [25] *to the only God our Savior be glory, majesty, power and authority, through Jesus Christ our Lord, before all ages, now and forevermore! Amen.*

Jude mentors the called-and-loved ones by providing principles to live by as they wage this contest for the faith and practice of Jesus Christ. Most churches today lock down on an expression or two for how each conceives of the Christian life. Their chosen expression is often catchy or poetic. In some churches their expression becomes a brand, while in others the expression emerged organically. Branding, the claim is, defines the church's mission, gives lurkers and observers and visitors a tagline to determine if that church is for them, and the brand can coordinate the various ministries of the church. Some claim branding provides a clearer idea for giving and potential donors. Many of us are not comfortable with too much branding in today's churches.

We can turn to texts like 1 Peter, 2 Peter, and Jude where we observe no attempt at reducing a church's mission or vision to a single expression. One could brand Jesus' moral vision, or Paul's, or John's, or the author of Hebrews', but none of them would satisfy the breadth and depth and width of their various terms. Major situations called forth fundamental principles, but by the time one is done reading the books one realizes no one expression does the job. Instead, each of these books uses a variety of expressions because each knows the specific term for the specific moment in that church at that time. So, I want to concentrate today's reading on four terms that bring to expression the Christian life in this letter: remember, keep yourselves, compassion for the doubting, and glorify God.

REMEMBER

In verse three, Jude expressed the mission contending for the faith, and in verse five that contest became a reminder of what the called-and-loved ones had absorbed as followers of Jesus. So, we are not surprised that in verse seventeen, as Jude begins to turn off his computer, the operative expression is "remember what the apostles of our Lord Jesus Christ foretold." To remember "refers to the mental and experiential

199

recall of God's act of salvation in Christ as made known through the apostles" (McKnight, "Jude," 1533).

The apostle most clearly in mind is Peter, and the utterance is found in 2 Peter 3:3, which reads "in the last days scoffers will come, scoffing and following their own desires." Or perhaps he has words of Paul in mind, like those in 2 Timothy 3:1–5. We may not have a firm grip on the specific apostle or a specific saying. The truth outweighs the specifics. Knowing the Christian tradition—our fathers and mothers in the faith, the basics of the faith, and the formative movements in our history—create pillars that extend from the Bible into our day and on which pillars we form gospel truths for our generation. A suggestion or two. Read a solid book on church history, and the book I recommend is Justo González, *The Story of Christianity*. It comes in two volumes. Read a chapter a week or a month and work your way through it. For no other reason than to become informed of the breadth, width, and depth of our family history. A solid way to remember our Christian faith is to read Michael Bird's *What Christians Ought to Believe*.

The big idea remains we can't "remember" or be "reminded" or "contend for the faith" if we have not first learned the faith and our family history.

KEEP YOURSELVES

Jude's second expression, which also forms connections to other lines in his letter, is "keep yourselves in God's love" and one does this "by building yourselves up in your most holy faith and praying in the Holy Spirit" (20–21). They are the called-and-loved ones (1–2, 17, 20) who are both "loved in God the Father" and "kept for Jesus Christ" (1), which is why they are to make every effort to "keep" or even guard themselves in that love. Being loved by God, loving God, loving oneself, and loving others are the deepest values of the Christian faith. It is the inner room that deserves to be locked and protected and guarded. The closest rival to that love is our love for our family—spouse and children and parents and siblings. Those loves are to be protected above all interpersonal relations, and even more protection is needed for divine love.

Jude instructs the called-and-loved ones to protect and keep that love by "forming yourselves on your most devout faith" (20; *Second Testament*), which is another way of saying "remember" (17). And they protect and keep that love by "praying in the Holy Spirit" (20). Jude may have in mind the Abba cry of the child's heart as we read in Galatians 4:6 ("God sent the Spirit of his Son into our hearts, the Spirit who calls out, '*Abba*, Father'"). Or he's referring to the common Christian experience that is described with "pray in the Spirit on all occasions" (Ephesians 6:18), which surely goes back to 5:18 where Paul instructed them to be "filled with the Spirit." This is both an experienced and an objective reality, but it is only fully known by those who have experienced it. This formation of the faith and protection of love are how to live "as you wait for the mercy of our Lord Jesus Christ to bring you to eternal life" (Jude 21). I recommend rereading 2 Peter 1:3–11 as a wonderful explanation of the time of waiting.

COMPASSION FOR THE DOUBTING

The redeemed are called to be agents of redemption. Jude does not put the final words on the end of this letter until he reminds them of their redemptive mission, and he does so with three expressions: be compassionate on the doubting, save some from the fires, and show compassion on such persons (22–23). One term used twice, but in two different ways: to be compassionate on those "who doubt" or who are "mentally wavering" (*Second Testament*) forms a companion with being compassionate on those need to be saved from fire. The NIV's decision to use semicolons creates separable instructions. I'm not so sure the various instructions in these two verses are to be separated. I will diagram them to show how they function in the original language, and I will use the *Second Testament*'s translation:

> Be compassionate to those mentally wavering,
>> Delivering them [mentally wavering]
>> Snatching them [mentally wavering] from fire
>> Be compassionate on those [mentally wavering]
>>> in awe
>> Hating even that robe stained from the flesh.

This diagram reveals that the first line carries the fundamental idea: they are to be compassionate or merciful to those who are mentally wavering, or who doubt. Who are these doubting? No doubt about it. They are those who are being attracted to the corrupted leaders who are described in verses three through nineteen. Which has a potent reminder for each of us: this text does not teach us to blast away at those who struggle with some bad ideas or who have lapsed into sensualities. This text warns the promoters of bad ideas and behaviors in severe language, but it flips the tone to compassion when it comes to the people of God who are being seduced by them. The wavering deserve care, not rebuke. Put in today's terms, the deconstructors deserve compassion and mercy and ears, not suspicion and condemnation.

Pastor Adam Hamilton has faced over the years both his own doubts and the doubts of others. No words better express what Jude means by "be compassionate" than these by Hamilton. He writes, "There was a time when, in meeting with people struggling with faith, I would have felt compelled to try to persuade them to believe. That seldom seemed helpful. What did seem helpful was to honestly admit there are legitimate questions that can be raised about faith; that there are things in the Bible that are troubling to thoughtful people; and that we all struggle with doubt, including me. I found that when I could articulate that I understood their questions, and that I, myself, had wrestled with some of these same questions and doubts over the last forty years, there was an openness to have a meaningful conversation about their doubts, and a greater openness to hear the reasons that, despite my doubts, I had faith" (Hamilton, *Wrestling with Doubt*, viii).

I join hands with Adam Hamilton, and here's why: I have myself faced doubt about passages in the Bible as well as some of the doctrines of the Christian faith. I have listened to some weighty saints of the church as they faced the dark sides of their faith. Most of us who have faced our doubts have continued to walk. But, at times our walking becomes limping, but we continue forward nevertheless, in faith and in hope.

Glorify God

Jude, like other New Testament letters, ends the day with a doxology, and Jude's is very much like two of the apostle Paul's:

> Now to him who is able to establish you in accordance with my gospel, the message I proclaim about Jesus Christ, in keeping with the revelation of the mystery hidden for long ages past. (Romans 16:25)

> Now to him who is able to do immeasurably more than all we ask or imagine, according to his power that is at work within us. (Ephesians 3:20)

But Jude elaborates his even more than Paul, and no doubt both of these "doxologists" were making use of the sort of doxology they heard in churches, which were rooted in doxologies in the Old Testament and synagogues (1 Chronicles 29:11). Jude effectively turns this doxology into a prayer.

The weight of Jude's doxology, which means giving glory to God, falls on God's keeping or protecting the called-and-loved ones. This divine protection is from "stumbling" (*Second Testament*) and for the purpose of making them stand "before his glorious presence" with an abundance of confident joy (24). Jude turns the doxology toward Jesus Christ, who is the Savior and who can deliver these called-and-loved ones from all that faces them (25). Which means Jude's doxology that begins in verse twenty-four with "to him who is able" is none other than "our only Deliverer-God "who delivers "through Jesus Christ."

This God deserves the praise and glory of the people of God.

Then.

And now.

And forever.

Doxologies, or benedictions like these mentioned, have been described as "being morphed" into worship together. As Walter Brueggemann describes it,

> And then we must leave and be morphed back to the way life was before. We return to our cars and have dinner at home or at the club, and we reengage family and have our usual joys and anxieties and quarrels and sex and war and the election and medical tests and appointments and movies . . ."

But, as he continues, "we are not morphed back to life the way it was; because everything has changed and reconfigured" when we were morphed into worship. Now, "we go back to life made new, as new as blessing, as new as Easter. We go back and be glad in obedience, a new name, a new peaceableness, a new miracle, a new discipleship, a new identity. The process of morphing claims that what happens here is not cut off when the service is over. The newness of God moves out with us, and we are blessed and we carry the power of blessing out with us. We leave the zone of holiness with a fresh glimpse of God's goodness." And this, too: "We do this over and over, because this new identity is not easily retained. But this new identity is our true joy and our true destiny" (Brueggemann, *Collected Sermons*, 279, 282–83).

Worship is a bit like entering into Narnia. Once you have been there—into the Narnia of worship—life is never the same again.

Questions for Reflection and Application

1. How much do you know about church history? Consider writing down a plan now to read a church history book as suggested.

2. Read about Jesus' compassion in the Gospels in Matthew 14:14, Matthew 20:34, Mark 1:40–41, Mark 6:34, and Luke 7:13. How do you think Jesus' example influenced his brother Jude's teachings on compassion?

3. Read Zechariah 3:1–5 and underline or take note of terms that are the same or similar. How could Zechariah have influenced Jude's language in verses 22–23?

4. When have you felt doubts about your faith, the Bible, doctrine, or church experiences? What kind of response did you need from Christians around you during those times?

5. At the end of this study, consider writing a doxology of your own. What do you want to express to God and about God, with worship, based on what you have learned here?

FOR FURTHER READING

Michael Bird, *What Christians Ought to Believe: An Introduction to Christian Doctrine through The Apostles' Creed* (Grand Rapids: Zondervan Academic, 2016).

Walter Brueggemann, *The Collected Sermons of Walter Brueggemann* (Louisville: Westminster John Knox, 2011).

Justo González, *The Story of Christianity*, 2 volumes (New York: HarperOne, 2010).

Adam Hamilton, *Wrestling with Doubt, Finding Faith* (Nashville: Abingdon, 2023).

New Testament Everyday
Bible Study Series

Become a daily Bible reader attentive to the mind of God

In the New Testament Everyday Bible Study Series, each volume:
- offers brief expositions of the biblical text and offers a clear focus for the central message of each passage;
- brings the passage alive with fresh images and what it means to follow King Jesus;
- provides biblical connections and questions for reflection and application for each passage.

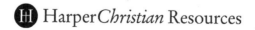

HarperChristian Resources

The Blue Parakeet, 2nd Edition

Rethinking How You Read the Bible

Scot McKnight, author of
The Jesus Creed

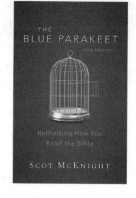

How are we to live out the Bible today? In this updated edition of *The Blue Parakeet*, you'll be challenged to see how Scripture transcends culture and time, and you'll learn how to come to God's Word with a fresh heart and mind.

The gospel is designed to be relevant in every culture, in every age, in every language. It's fully capable of this, and, as we read Scripture, we are called to discern how God is speaking to us today.

And yet applying its words and directions on how to live our lives is not as easy as it seems. As we talk to the Christians around us about issues that matter, many of us wonder: how on earth are we reading the same Bible? How is it that two of us can sit down with the same Bible and come away with two entirely different answers about everything from charismatic gifts to the ordaining of women?

Professor and author of *The King Jesus Gospel* Scot McKnight challenges us to rethink how to read the Bible, not just to puzzle it together into some systematic belief or historical tradition but to see it as an ongoing Story that we're summoned to enter and to carry forward in our day.

What we need is a fresh blowing of God's Spirit on our culture, in our day, and in our ways. We need twenty-first-century Christians living out the biblical gospel in twenty-first-century ways. And if we read the Bible properly, we will see that God never asked one generation to step back in time and live in ways of the past.

Through the Bible, God speaks in each generation, in that generation's ways and beckons us to be a part of his amazing story.

Available in stores and online!

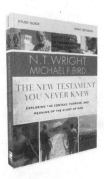
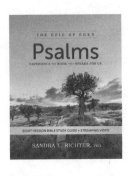
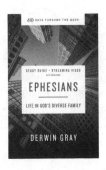

Following King Jesus

We want to follow King Jesus, but do we know how?

Author and professor Scot McKnight will help you discover what it means to follow King Jesus through 24 lessons based on four of his writings (*The King Jesus Gospel*, *The Blue Parakeet - 2nd edition*, *One.Life*, and *A Fellowship of Differents*). McKnight's unique framework for discipleship is designed to be used for personal study and within disciple-making groups of two or more. In this workbook, McKnight will help you:

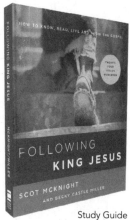

Study Guide
9780310105992

- Know the biblical meaning of the gospel
- Read the Bible and understand how to apply it today
- Live as disciples of Jesus in all areas of life
- Show the world God's character through life together in the church

Each lesson, created by Becky Castle Miller, has both Personal Study and Group Discussion sections. The Personal Study section contains a discipleship reading from Scot McKnight, an insightful Bible study, an insightful Bible study, and a time for individual prayer, action, and reflection. The Group Discussion section includes discussion questions and activities to do together with a discipleship group. You'll share insights from your personal study time with each other and explore different ways of living out what you're learning.

Whether you have been a Christian for many years or you are desiring a fresh look at what it means to be a disciple, this workbook is an in-depth guide to what it means to follow King Jesus and to discover how to put that kind of life into practice.

HarperChristian Resources